D0903036

No Uncertain Sound

Reformed Doctrine and Life

REFORMEDFORUM

Reformed Forum
P. O. Box 27422
Philadelphia, PA 19118
www.reformedforum.org

Scripture quotations are from the ESV® Bible (The Holy Bible, English Standard Version®), copyright © 2001 by Crossway, a publishing ministry of Good News Publishers. Used by permission. All rights reserved.

ISBN: 978-0-9987487-0-2 (paperback)
         978-0-9987487-1-9 (ebook)

Abbreviations

ESV   English Standard Version Bible
KJV   King James Version Bible
WCF   Westminster Confession of Faith
WJE   The Works of Jonathan Edwards
WSC   Westminster Shorter Catechism
WLC   Westminster Larger Catechism
WTJ   The Westminster Theological Journal

CONTENTS

INTRODUCTION

For if the trumpet give an uncertain sound, who shall prepare himself to the battle? So likewise you, except ye utter by the tongue words easy to be understood, how shall it be known what is spoken? for ye shall speak into the air. —1 Corinthians 14:8–9 KJV

Him we proclaim, warning everyone and teaching everyone with all wisdom, that we may present everyone mature in Christ. —Colossians 1:28 ESV

REFORMED FORUM EXISTS to assist the church in her call to discipleship. We serve the church by communicating the riches of our theological tradition and advancing it according to our confessional boundaries through in-depth research and scholarly discourse. We occupy a narrow niche within the Christian church, and this book serves as a manifesto of sorts. There are many faithful Christian organizations committed to advancing the gospel, yet we are distinct, and we desire to issue a clear call—no uncertain sound—to those with ears to hear.

We believe that the Word of God, which is contained in the inerrant and infallible Scriptures of the Old and New Testaments, is the ultimate authority for faith and practice. We also subscribe to the Westminster Confession of Faith and Catechisms as our secondary standards. These standards contain the system of doctrine shared by our churches. While we stand upon Scripture first, and this confessional tradition second, the chapters ahead establish Reformed Forum's unique timbre, a distinct theological voice. Reformed Forum is neither mainline nor evangelical; Reformed Forum is confessionally Reformed and Presbyterian.

2

As Calvinists, we believe one must be regenerated, that is, "born again," to be saved. We unite our hearts and voices with evangelicals who confess that salvation is strictly by grace alone through faith alone in Jesus Christ alone. But "evangelicalism," especially since the 1940s, has advocated for other beliefs. Charlie Dennison, former historian for the Orthodox Presbyterian Church, expresses our conviction well,

> Some have had trouble understanding the aversion that others have to evangelicalism. They have been unable to accept the conclusion of Cornelius Van Til and others that evangelicalism, as a system, is Arminian. They have been unable to accept the criticism that modern evangelicalism's view of regeneration is subjective, incapable of rising above a personal experience of sin and grace to the level of the covenant and the federal headship of Adam and Christ. Further, they have been unable to accept the growing historical and social evidence that contemporary evangelicalism is worldly, individualistic, and adolescent, craving acceptance and desperately wanting to make an impact.[1]

We desire to be faithful to Christ and to be good stewards of the resources and opportunities he has provided. While we desire to see his kingdom advance in this world, our sole aim is to please him rather than gain broad acceptance from the culture. Dennison continues,

> Modern practical theology, however, has moved in a man-centered direction, having adopted a worldly agenda for remedial goals and perceivable gains. Growth and year-end statistics have become gods. Christian maturity is confused with the mastery of methods, managerial skills, and the ability to cope. Modern practical theology trivializes the biblical vision by exalting incidental matters to the level of greatest concern. This is usually done, sometimes unwittingly, through a blend of social sciences, religious technology, and commercialism. In its more tragic expressions, it is ridiculous.[2]

Reformed Forum supports the church by providing resources. While we are privy to new methods of communication and publication, we recognize that Jesus Christ builds his church primarily through the ordi-

---

1. Charles G. Dennison, "Some Thoughts about Our Identity" in *History for a Pilgrim People: The Historical Writings of Charles G. Dennison*, ed. Danny E. Olinger and David K. Thompson (Willow Grove, Penn.: The Committee for the Historian of the Orthodox Presbyterian Church, 2002), 204.
2. Ibid., 205–206.

nary means of grace: the ministries of the Word, sacrament, and prayer. There are no "new measures" to guarantee the advancement of the kingdom, no other recipes to make disciples. This book is our attempt to set forth the salient features of our Reformed identity.

Lane G. Tipton establishes our redemptive-historical approach to the Scriptures with an essay on Jesus in the Old Testament. He demonstrates that the Scriptures of the Old Testament presuppose a progressive, organic, revelation of the Messiah in promise form that gives way to eschatological fulfillment in the humiliation and exaltation of Jesus Christ. Christ is not an afterthought. The church must receive the Christ who is truly revealed in the Scriptures of the Old and New Testaments by the supernatural agency of the Spirit. He speaks powerfully in Scripture as a revelational record of the history of special revelation.

Camden M. Bucey builds upon Tipton's work by demonstrating our belief in the relationship between biblical and systematic theology. These two disciplines inform and regulate one another. While both are based on exegetical theology, systematic theology organizes the teaching of Scripture topically while biblical theology studies Scripture as it progressively unfolds. We believe a true Reformed theologian must not only be systematic but also biblical-theological.

Jeffrey C. Waddington addresses the doctrine of salvation with his chapter on union with Christ and the *ordo salutis*. Nothing is more significant about a Christian than the fact that he is united to Christ. The good news is that the triune God has brought us into a blessed relationship, a covenantal communion bond with him through his Son. We have every Spiritual blessing in the heavenly places *in Christ* (Eph 1:3). In accord with that glorious truth, Glen J. Clary reminds us that Reformed theology is not merely intellectual. It has bearing upon our practice. We were created to glorify and enjoy God forever, and therefore Reformed theology must be directed toward worship. Furthermore, God has instructed us *how* to worship. By following his Word, we experience his grace and grow ever closer to him.

Our identity is hidden away with Christ in God. Yet Jesus calls us to be salt and light in the world. As such, we are separatist though not isolationist.[3] James J. Cassidy explains this existence. We are citizens of

3. Here we employ language adopted by Rev. John P. Galbraith, former General Secretary for the Committee on Home Missions and Church Extension as well as the

heaven and not of this world. We are pilgrims traveling through the wilderness unto the Promised Land, our eternal rest in the New Heavens and New Earth. Cassidy develops an ecclesiology and ethic of heavenly-mindedness. We are in a war, but "we do not wrestle against flesh and blood, but against the rulers, against the authorities, against the cosmic powers over this present darkness, against the spiritual forces of evil in the heavenly places" (Eph 6:12). As such, we fight not with the weapons of this world, but with the weapons of Christ's heavenly kingdom.

Jeffrey C. Waddington directs us in this fight with a concluding chapter about Reformed apologetics. Peter says we must always be prepared to make a defense to anyone who asks you for a reason for the hope that is in us (1 Pet 3:15). Paul says we are to take every thought captive to the obedience of Christ (2 Cor 10:5). There is no neutrality. We defend the faith on the basis of the self-attesting Word of God. We seek to share the uncompromised message of Christ crucified and raised for sinners. We hope this book will facilitate the spread of this message. As more people read it and study these matters closely, we pray that Christ would enlist more soldiers in our churches to fight the good fight of the faith (1 Tim 6:12).

Committee on Foreign Missions of the Orthodox Presbyterian Church. Rev. Galbraith labored for years to establish ecumenical relationships across denominational boundaries. We advocate cooperation among Christians and strong ecumenical relations wherever the confessional standards of churches permit. Nonetheless, our eccesiastical identity is not bound up with a continuing church. Listen to our audio documentary on Rev. Galbraith at http://reformedforum.org/ctc441.

THE ROOTS OF
REFORMED FORUM

CAMDEN M. BUCEY

MY PERSONAL HISTORY loosely parallels the experience of many early "fundamentalists," including J. Gresham Machen, who left the mainline Presbyterian Church in the United States of America to form what would become the Orthodox Presbyterian Church in 1936. In his battle with theological liberalism, Machen came to an awareness that he could no longer support his own denomination. His ecclesiastical home for many years had changed, and Machen and his strong convictions were no longer welcome.

I was raised in the same rural church as my father and grandmother in Stillman Valley, a small town in northern Illinois. We have deep roots there. When I was born, Kishwaukee Community Presbyterian Church was a member of the United Presbyterian Church in the United States of America. In 1983, it merged with the southern Presbyterian Church in the United States (PCUS) to form the Presbyterian Church (USA), the mainline church we know today. My local church was conservative on many fronts, holding to the inspiration, inerrancy, and infallibility of the Scriptures. I heard the gospel of grace each Lord's Day. Still, I was not catechized nor was I conversant with the doctrines of grace, even though my pastor was a five-point Calvinist.

From Evangelical to Reformed

During my undergraduate studies at Bradley University, in Peoria, Illinois, I became involved with Campus Crusade for Christ. Amid this formative time, I studied my Bible and was exposed to a wide range of theological positions. I had never heard of an earthly millennial kingdom or a rapture, and I had no idea what to make of them. Despite growing up in the church, I had no doctrinal framework to help me understand and evaluate these claims. I also came into explicit contact with Calvinist soteriology. The first time I heard that salvation ultimately depends on God's sovereign choice rather than man's free will, I was vehemently (and loudly) opposed. But over the months and years I started to grow in my understanding. As I continued to read and study the Bible, I was changing.

I started attending Bethany Baptist Church in Peoria, and I heard the gospel clearly there. The pastoral staff faithfully taught the doctrines of grace and preached well-crafted expository sermons. The church had a heart for the Bible and discipleship. At Bethany I met Chris Jenkins, who served as the family pastor. He was also a PhD student at Trinity Evangelical Divinity School in Deerfield, Illinois, some three hours away. On days when he didn't have class, I often met with Chris to discuss theology. Chris introduced me to the apologetics of Cornelius Van Til. I was hooked. After learning that Van Til taught at Westminster Theological Seminary in Philadelphia, I discovered the school's pre-seminary reading list and dedicated my nights and weekends for the next few years.

While I could meet with Chris occasionally, he was busy with pastoral ministry, PhD studies, and a young family. He was more than generous with his time and patient with an eager neophyte. Still, I yearned for more opportunities to discuss theology. I wanted a regular discussion group. I could talk theology all night. Chris ran Sola Gratia Ministries, a collection of online resources at solagratia.org. I began working on the website, developing a rudimentary content management system and formatting articles for the site. We also started a blog, which was a relatively new thing, especially in the world of Reformed theology. Chris and I quickly realized it would be beneficial to have other people contribute to the blog. We did not know who to ask, so we blindly emailed Bill Edgar, Professor of Apologetics at Westminster Theological Seminary. He gave us the names of two PhD students who might be interested in the project: Sebastian Heck and Jeff Waddington. Jeff and Sebastian wrote several articles for the site, and we started to gain more traction in the online community. While I did not realize it at the time, I was developing a relationship that would extend well beyond a blog.

Throughout this time, I sensed the Lord calling me to gospel ministry. After taking a few distance courses, I decided to begin studying full-time at Westminster Theological Seminary. In the spring of 2007, my wife, Erica, and I visited Philadelphia to find an apartment. I called Jeff to let him know I would be in town, and he invited me to a meeting of the Das & Kees Society,[1] a student group that would gather to discuss books and articles in the tradition of Machen and Van Til. This time they planned to gather at Dr. Lane Tipton's house. I had never heard of him; nevertheless, I thought it would be great to meet Jeff in person and spend some time with other people from Westminster. We discussed Van Til's apologetic, and I felt so energized. This was the kind of theological discussion I had been yearning for all those years in Peoria.

That summer, Erica and I moved to Philadelphia. She began working at the Sunday Breakfast Rescue Mission while I took up with summer Hebrew. We joined Calvary Orthodox Presbyterian Church in Glenside, Pennsylvania and began developing many friendships with people at church and at the seminary. It was soon thereafter that Jeff introduced me to Jim Cassidy, a minister at Calvary OPC in Ringoes, New Jersey and a PhD student at the seminary.

From Castle Church to Reformed Forum

It is debatable when the podcast was invented. By 2005, the idea of enclosing mp3 files in an RSS feed was catching on in the tech community. I had been listening to podcasts for a couple of years, well before Apple started supporting podcasts with iTunes (and years before smart phones). I had to download the mp3 from the website and then manually transfer the file to my iPod using a USB cable. Rudimentary

---

1. Das and Kees (pronounced "case") were the nicknames of J. Gresham Machen and Cornelius Van Til, respectively.

software existed for automating the download portion, but the syncing was always a hassle. It was less than ideal, but I did it every morning and listened to podcasts like *This Week in Tech* and sermons from Desiring God.

After a semester at Westminster, my tech side started to fuse with my theological side. I began thinking how much I enjoyed the frequent and stimulating theological conversations. I also realized other people did not have these opportunities. I was one of those people while living in Peoria. And so I approached Jeff and Jim about recording our conversations and releasing them as a podcast. We had no significant barriers to overcome. As a guitar player, I already owned some recording gear that could be used for podcasting. We just needed to select a topic and schedule a recording. Our first recording was a discussion on the New Testament's use of the Old Testament. I recorded from home, while Jim and Jeff connected over Skype. Our second recording covered building a theological library. It lasted for over two hours, and I decided to split it into two parts. I didn't know what I was doing with the editing software, and it took me longer to edit than it took for us to record. A few months later we recorded an episode on Van Til's theology from a bedroom in Jeff's old apartment in Wyndmoor, Pennsylvania. To appropriate Peter Steiner's famous *New Yorker* cartoon, when you're a podcaster, no one knows you're recording from a closet.[2]

From day one, we settled on the name *Christ the Center* for our flagship program, but if you listen to those early recordings, you will hear us mention CastleChurch.org. This was a domain name I owned from a previous project. It was an homage to the *Schloßkirche* in Wittenberg where Luther nailed his ninety-five theses. Regrettably, the name was confusing, and several people thought we were a church. In 2008 we changed our name to Reformed Forum and purchased our domain ReformedForum.org. With the help of our friend James Sweet, we incorporated under the new name on April 1, 2010, and were recognized as a 501(c)(3) tax-exempt non-profit organization by the IRS several months later.[3] While we continued to work on a shoestring budget and had very little production experience, the Lord blessed our efforts.

---

2. Steiner's panel shows a dog on a computer, explaining to another that, "On the Internet, no one knows you're a dog." *The New Yorker*, July 5, 1993.

3. The irony of incorporating on April Fool's Day is not lost upon us.

In 2008, Jeff co-edited *Resurrection and Eschatology: Theology in Service of the Church: Essays in Honor of Richard B. Gaffin, Jr.*[1] with Lane Tipton. On our twenty-second episode, released June 20, 2008, we welcomed Lane as our first guest to speak about the festschrift. Other guests would follow shortly thereafter, including Lane Keister (ep. 23), Gary Johnson (ep. 24), R. Scott Clark (ep. 27), Ligon Duncan (ep. 28), and Derek Thomas (ep. 29). As the months went by, word spread and more people listened. We started adding panelists. Nick Batzig joined us in June 2008 for episode 21 and James Dolezal joined nearly a month later in episode 24. Glen Clary first appeared as a guest on episode 75 (June 26, 2009). Jared Oliphint and Jonathan Brack participated in an entertaining episode 100 (December 11, 2009) in which we debated paedobaptism with our friend Bob LaRocca. As more people began to contribute, we added new programs, including *Reformed Media Review* and *Philosophy for Theologians*. Though we were growing and more people were involved, we always sought to remain true to our identity.

---

1. Lane G. Tipton and Jeffrey C. Waddington, *Resurrection and Eschatology: Theology in Service of the Church: Essays in Honor of Richard B. Gaffin, Jr.* (Phillipsburg, N.J.: P&R Publishing, 2008).

3

JESUS IN THE OLD TESTAMENT

THE HISTORY OF APOSTOLIC IMAGINATION OR THE HISTORY OF SPECIAL REVELATION?

LANE G. TIPTON

OW HAS THE Reformed tradition understood Jesus Christ in relation to the Old Testament Scriptures? What are the hermeneutical assumptions involved in relating Jesus to the Old Testament? What presuppositions about the nature of the history of special revelation come into view? How are we to understand the nature of the "grammar" and "history" recorded in the Old Testament that has Christ as its central subject matter? Exactly how should we understand terms such as "grammatical-historical interpretation," "Christocentrism," and "Christotelism"?

For purposes of introduction, it is best to understand Christocentrism as the tenet that Christ is the central redemptive subject matter of the Old Testament, understood on its own terms, quite apart from the New Testament Scriptures. Christotelism is best understood to entail that Christ is the consummate *telos* of what the Old Testament Scriptures promise, namely, a crucified and resurrected Messiah. The christocentric and the christotelic require one another and mutually contextualize one another; the one does not exist apart from the other.

A corollary of the conjunction of Christocentrism and Christotelism is that the grammar and history of the Old Testament Scriptures are a function of the history of special revelation—a progressive and historical revelation that has the Son of God as its central subject matter that moves toward realization in the death and resurrection of Jesus Christ. As such, the grammar and history presented in the Old Testament Scriptures is a Christ-centered and Christ-focused history of special revelation.

To put the matter a bit differently, it is not "bare" or exclusively human grammar and history that is contained in the Old Testament. It is rather a revelational record of the history of special revelation that has the triune God as its author and Christ as its central subject matter. Thus, whatever we say about grammatical-historical interpretation and ascertaining the historical context and human authorial intention of a given Old Testament passage, we must situate the grammatical-historical method in the more basic category of the history of special revelation.

The basic thesis of this brief essay is that the Scriptures of the Old Testament presuppose a progressive, organic, revelation of the Messiah in promise form that gives way to eschatological fulfillment in the humiliation and exaltation of Jesus Christ. In order to make clear the theological and hermeneutical assumptions that make possible a Christ-centered (Christocentric) and Christ-directed (Christotelic) Old Testament, we will examine in survey form a number of biblical texts and seek to relate these texts to formulations within the confessionally Reformed tradition. With these basic, introductory observations in place, let us examine the methodological assumptions that render intelligible a robust Christ-centered understanding of the Old Testament, particularly in light of recent proposals that depart from a through-going Christ-centered understanding of the Old Testament.

Critical or Historicist Christotelic Methodology

In order to move toward a positive presentation of a biblical, reformed view of Christ in the Old Testament, it will prove instructive to explore what, from a biblical perspective, is an inadequate and, in fact, deviant approach that seeks to relate Christ to the Old Testament Scriptures. That approach can be found in the work of Peter Enns. Enns' species of Christotelism represents a fundamental departure from the historic

Reformed understanding that Christ is presented in the *per se* witness of the Old Testament.

The Enns view, or perhaps better, the Enns-McCartney view,[1] can be termed Critical Christotelism (or Historicist Christotelism). This approach asserts that the Old Testament, on its own terms and in light of a grammatical-historical "first reading," cannot sustain a typological reading that is Christ-centered. That is, the Old Testament is not intrinsically centered on the kingdom, person, and work of Christ; the Old Testament is a history of the religion of an ancient Hebrew people. Typology, a reading of the Old Testament that construes it as both revealing and anticipating Christ in provisional forms, is only recognized in terms of a retrospective "second reading" of the Old Testament in light of its surprise fulfillment in Christ. Once Christ unexpectedly appears, then, and only then, can we read the Old Testament again and recognize an *ex post facto* typological strand that is not resident in the Old Testament on its own terms (i.e., on its own grammatical-historical terms).

Further, Enns, in an article entitled "Apostolic Hermeneutics and an Evangelical Doctrine of Scripture: Moving Beyond a Modernist Impasse,"[2] argued that there is no meaningful difference between the method by which the Apostles read the Old Testament and the way that Second Temple Jews read the Old Testament. All Second Temple methods of interpretation understand the Old Testament in light of its alleged fulfillment within the experience of the second temple community reading the Old Testament. The Apostles used this method and,

---

1. See, for example, Peter Enns, "Fuller Meaning, Single Goal: A Christotelic Approach to the New Testament Use of the Old in Its First-Century Interpretive Environment" in *Three Views on the New Testament Use of the Old Testament*, K. Berding and J. Lunde, eds. (Grand Rapids: Zondervan, 2008), 167–217, and Dan G. McCartney, "Should We Employ the Hermeneutics of the New Testament Writers?" (Annual Meeting of the Evangelical Theological Society, Atlanta, Georgia, 2003). See also my critiques of these views in "Christocentrism *and* Christotelism: The Spirit, Redemptive History, and the Gospel" (forthcoming), and "The Gospel and Redemptive-Historical Hermeneutics" in John R. Muether and Danny E. Olinger, eds., *Confident of Better Things: Essays Commemorating 75 Years of the Orthodox Presbyterian Church* (Willow Grove, Pennsylvania: Committee for the Historian of the Orthodox Presbyterian Church, 2011), 185–213. I will merely summarize their views, based in part on these resources, just cited.

2. Peter Enns, "Apostolic Hermeneutics and an Evangelical Doctrine of Scripture: Moving Beyond a Modernist Impasse," *The Westminster Theological Journal* 65, no. 2 (2003): 263–288.

just as arbitrarily as any other Second Temple Jew, interpreted the text in light of the New Testament community experience. In their case, it was their "experience" of Christ. Bruce Waltke summarizes the view of Second Temple Judaism that Enns imposes on the Apostles,

> New Testament writers used stories invented during the Second Temple period as a basis for theology; and that they employed the highly arbitrary *pesher* method of interpretation, which was used in IQpHab. According to this method of interpretation, the people who believe they are living in the eschaton *impose their convictions on reluctant Old Testament texts.*[3]

In *Inspiration and Incarnation*, Enns advances this very approach and asserts that for the NT authors "Christ gives the Old Testament final coherence,"[4] but only as they look at the Old Testament "in a *whole new light*" that bypasses "what the Old Testament author intended."[5] The net effect of this method is that Christ comes to be related to the Old Testament in terms of an enormously imaginative, apostolic re-reading of the Old Testament toward Christ. Christ is not intrinsically revealed in the Old Testament Scriptures. He is rather inserted into the Old Testament by means of apostolic imagination. The Old Testament, in the words of Walter Brueggemann, is an "elusive, polyphonic text" and, as such, requires an "imaginative construal of the Old Testament toward Jesus" in order to confer upon it a Christological sense.[6]

A Reformed Assessment of Critical Christotelism

Enns' "Christotelic" view was not only propagated in print, but, more controversially, in the classroom while teaching Old Testament at Westminster Theological Seminary from the mid 1990s through 2008. Clair Davis, for instance, lauds Enns' "Christotelic" approach as the constructive way forward for biblical theology in the tradition of Geerhardus Vos. Others, such as Richard B. Gaffin, Jr., understand that the

3. Bruce Waltke, *An Old Testament Theology: An Exegetical, Canonical, and Thematic Approach* (Grand Rapids, Mich.: Zondervan, 2007), 34n18 (emphasis added).

4. Peter Enns, *Inspiration and Incarnation: Evangelicals and the Problem of the Old Testament* (Grand Rapids, Mich.: Baker, 2005), 160.

5. Ibid. (emphasis added).

6. Walter Brueggemann, *Old Testament Theology: Testimony, Dispute, Advocacy* (Minneapolis, Fortress Press: 1997), 732.

Enns-McCartney hermeneutic is a departure from not only Vos, but from historic Reformed theology and hermeneutics. Gaffin, in a response to Davis, observes that,

> the controversy that began to engulf the Seminary around 2006, that at stake are two contending understandings of biblical theology, the one for whom Vos can be said to be the father, the other a more recent and diverging conception, associated with a "Christotelic" interpretation, which, as far as Vos is concerned, understands itself as needing to go "beyond Vos," particularly in his reading of the Old Testament perceived as (too) "flat."[7]

Gaffin cites two rather lengthy quotations from Vos in order to make the point that what Vos opposed in his day seems to be for all practical purposes Enns' conception of Christotelism. The quotations are taken from Vos' "Hebrews, the Epistle of the Diatheke,"[8] written in 1916,

---

7. Richard B. Gaffin, Jr., "WRF Member Westminster Theological Seminary Responds to Clair Davis' Comments Regarding the 'Retirement' of Doug Green," Text, *World Reformed Fellowship*, (June 30, 2014), http://wrfnet.org/articles/2014/06/wrf-member-westminster-theological-seminary-responds-clair-daviss-comments.

8. "Reformed theology has with greater earnestness than any other type of Christian doctrine upheld the principles of the absoluteness and unchanging identity of truth. It is the most anti-pragmatic of all forms of Christian teaching. And this is all the more remarkable since it has from the beginning shown itself possessed of a true historic sense in the apprehension of the progressive character of the deliverance of truth. Its doctrine of the covenants on its historical side represents the first attempt at constructing a history of revelation and may justly be considered the precursor of what is at present called biblical theology. But the Reformed have always insisted upon it that at no point shall a recognition of the historical delivery and apprehension of truth be permitted to degenerate into a relativity of truth. The history remains a history of revelation. Its total product agrees absolutely in every respect with the sum of truth as it lies in the eternal mind and purpose of God. If already the religion of the Old and New Testament church was identical, while the process of supernatural revelation was still going on, how much more must the church, since God has spoken for the last time in His Son, uphold the ideal absoluteness of her faith as guaranteed by its agreement with the Word of God that abideth forever. It is an unchristian and an unbiblical procedure to make development superior to revelation instead of revelation superior to development, to accept belief and tendencies as true because they represent the spirit of the time and in a superficial optimism may be regarded as making for progress. Christian cognition is not an evolution of truth, but a fallible apprehension of truth which must at each point be tested by an accessible absolute norm of truth. To take one's stand upon the infallibility of the Scriptures is an eminently religious act; it honors the supremacy of God in the sphere of truth in the same way as the author of Hebrews does by insisting upon it, notwithstanding all progress, that the Old and the New Testament are the same authoritative speech of God." Geerhardus Vos, "Hebrews, the Epistle of the Diatheke" in *Redemptive History*

and "The Idea of Biblical Theology as a Science and as a Theological Discipline,"[9] written in 1894.

Gaffin notes that Vos establishes a distinctive conception of how the historical progress of special revelation interfaces with the absolute character of such revealed truth. The progressive character of the history of special revelation is not set in opposition to its absolute and unchanging identity. Gaffin observes,

> The epoch-making stature of Vos is not in drawing attention for the first time to the significance of the fundamentally historical nature of revelation, though his work certainly highlights that—especially important where it is missed or underappreciated. Rather, his singular importance is in opening the way, in a post-Enlightenment setting, to biblically sound alternatives in the face of the destructive biblical theologies spawned by the historical-critical method in the late 18th and throughout the 19th centuries down to his own time.[10]

Put differently, Gaffin argues that "Vos is concerned to stress that within Scripture and the history of revelation (of which the origin of Scripture is a part) the historical character of its truth, while integral, is subordinate to its revealed character." Hence, while the "historical development is essential, revelation, as he says, is 'supreme.'" Gaffin then relates Vos' insights to the Ennsian Christotelic approach as follows:

> It is this point of the entire truthfulness of the history of revelation and Scripture—involving "the truth, the whole truth, and nothing but the truth," as Vos says, and critically essential for any doctrine of

---

and Biblical Interpretation: The Shorter Writings of Geerhardus Vos, Richard B. Gaffin, Jr., ed. (Phillipsburg, NJ: P & R Publishing, 2001), 232–233.

9. "The second point to be emphasized in our treatment of Biblical Theology is that the historical character of the truth is not in any way antithetical to, but throughout subordinated to, its revealed character. Scriptural truth is not absolute, notwithstanding its historic setting; but the historic setting has been employed by God for the very purpose of revealing the truth, the whole truth, and nothing but the truth. It is not the duty of Biblical Theology to seek first the historic features of the Scriptural ideas, and to think that the absolute character of the truth as revealed of God is something secondary to be added thereunto. The reality of revelation should be the supreme factor by which the historic factor is kept under control. With the greatest variety of historical aspects, there can, nevertheless, be no inconsistencies or contradictions in the Word of God." Geerhardus Vos, "The Idea of Biblical Theology as a Science and as a Theological Discipline" in *Redemptive History and Biblical Interpretation: The Shorter Writings of Geerhardus Vos*, Richard B. Gaffin, Jr., ed. (Phillipsburg, NJ: P & R Publishing, 2001), 19.

10. Gaffin, Jr., "Response to Clair Davis."

Scripture, like that set out in chapter 1 of the WCF, intent on doing justice to the unity and coherent harmony of the Bible as God's own written word—it is just this crucially important point that is compromised or at best obscured by the Christotelic approach to Scripture. This happens through its "first read–second read" treatment of the Old Testament that it adopts. The first read seeks to establish the original historical meaning or original human author meaning of an Old Testament passage on its own terms without any reference to the New Testament. The second read of the passage then seeks to show how in the light of the New Testament it is about Christ, to disclose its Christotelic content. This approach as a whole is ill-conceived and seriously flawed.[11]

Gaffin quickly adds that for Vos the issue of whether Old Testament authors understood "all this in detail is not relevant," because "without doubt, they would have grasped the heart of the matter."[12]

All of this means that the Old Testament authors understood the essentially Christ-centered character of the history of special revelation as it moved progressively toward its consummation in Christ Himself. As a result of these observations, their words (grammar) and the history of which they wrote (historical) are subsumed under a history of special revelation that has Christ as its central redemptive subject matter and consummative *telos*. Gaffin's insights therefore have significant implications for enriching the grammatical-historical method in the service of the history of a Christ-centered revelation. To sum up, Vos' formulation yields a view of Christotelism (Christ as consummate *telos*) that depends at this very point on Christ being the central redemptive subject matter of the Old Testament on its own terms (Christocentrism).

Exegetical and Theological Considerations

Gaffin lists a number of biblical texts that bear out Vos' formulations (e.g., Luke 24:44–45; John 5:39–47; 8:56; 12:41; 1 Pet 1:10–12) and at the same time expose the problems with Enns' Historicist Christotelic approach. First, as an orienting observation to understanding the nature of biblical revelation, the Scriptures of the Old and New Testaments are the deposit through which we hear the Spirit speaking

---

11. Ibid.
12. Ibid.

to the church. As 2 Tim 3:16 and 2 Pet 1:19–20 make clear, the Scriptures, as God-breathed, are a revelation from God. They are of divine produce. As such, in the language of the Westminster Confession of Faith, the church is to rest in "no other but the *Holy Spirit speaking in the Scripture.*"[13] This is critical to understand, because the Scriptures are essentially a Word from God, and in them we hear the Spirit speaking. We do not hear in the New Testament an errant human voice of an interpretive (Second Temple) community, who has re-imagined the Old Testament around its experience in Christ. Rather, we hear the Spirit interpreting in the New Testament what the Spirit revealed in the Old Testament.

Second, and building on this point, both Paul and Peter make explicit the divine authorship of the Scripture as it roots the gospel of God's Son in the *per se* witness of the Old Testament, and in a way that was sufficiently understood by the human authors of the Old Testament. Paul asserts that the gospel is the gospel of God (Rom 1:1) that concerns His Son (Rom 1:3a). This gospel is promised beforehand by God through his prophets in the Old Testament Scriptures (Rom 1:2) and reaches its consummate fulfillment in the death and resurrection of Jesus Christ (Rom 1:3–4). Peter makes explicit that "the Spirit of Christ" in the prophets "predicted in advance the sufferings of Christ and the subsequent glories" (1 Pet 1:11). By the agency of the Spirit, breathing out the Scriptures (2 Tim 3:16), it was revealed to the prophets in the Old Covenant that they were serving "you"—the New Covenant church (1 Pet 1:12), "concerning this salvation" (v. 9a), understood as "the grace that was to be yours" (v. 9b), "through those who preached the gospel to you by the Holy Spirit sent from heaven" (v. 12b). Old Covenant prophets understood the sufferings of the Christ and the subsequent glories by virtue of the supernatural, revelatory agency of the Spirit of Christ in them. Commenting on 1 Peter 1:10–12, Gaffin observes, "the intense interest of the Old Testament prophets as a whole was in what *'the Spirit of Christ' at work in them was disclosing about his own eventual coming, his sufferings and consequent glory* (1 Pet 1:10–11)."[14]

Historicist Christotelism of the Ennsian variety has replaced the revelatory agency of the Holy Spirit with the so-called imagination of the

---

13. Westminster Confession of Faith, 1:10 (emphasis added).
14. Ibid. (emphasis added).

Apostles. But to read 1 Pet 1:11 in this way would actually undermine the truth of what Peter asserts, because on the Enns-McCartney view, Peter is simply re-interpreting the Old Testament as though the Spirit of Christ predicted and revealed in advance such things, when, in fact, He did not. First Peter 1:11 on the historicist view of Enns and company, would be one more example of an already re-imagined Old Testament. But it could not be clearer that, in opposition to the claims from those like Enns, McCartney and Brueggemann, the apostles interpret *an already Christ-centered and Christ-directed gospel of Jesus Christ, because they write by the inspiration of the same Spirit who revealed the same gospel to the prophets.* The ultimate root of Historicist Christotelism is unbelief, wrapped in a critical conception of history, as some species of Kantian phenomena that cannot accommodate a Christocentric history of special revelation.

Third, and in the light of these observations, certain passages in the New Testament, like Luke 24:25–27 and John 5:39–47, make it abundantly clear that Jesus held people accountable for failing to see what the Spirit revealed concerning Himself in the Old Testament Scriptures. He says to the Pharisees *prior to his resurrection* in John 5:39–40: "You search the Scriptures because you think that in them you have eternal life; and it is they that bear witness about me, yet you refuse to come to me that you may have life." He says to his disciples *after his resurrection* in Luke 24:25–27:

> And he said to them, "O foolish ones, and slow of heart to believe all that the prophets have spoken! Was it not necessary that the Christ should suffer these things and enter into his glory?" And beginning with Moses and all the Prophets, he interpreted to them in all the Scriptures the things concerning himself (Luke 24:25–27, ESV).

Whether Pharisee or disciple, whether prior to his resurrection or after his resurrection, Jesus holds accountable (as foolish and faithless) those who fail to see what the Spirit sufficiently and perspicuously revealed in the Old Testament Scripture concerning Himself.

Fourth, the previous point is made even stronger when we recognize that Old Testament saints understood the very things the Pharisees and disciples miss. Both Abraham and Isaiah, according to Jesus, understood what the Spirit had revealed concerning Himself. He says, "Your father Abraham rejoiced that he would see my day. He saw it and was glad" (John 8:56). Again, "Isaiah said this because he saw [Jesus'] glo-ry and spoke about him" (John 12:41). Not only did Isaiah speak (or write) but also, in speaking, he himself saw or understood. Note the syntax of verse 41. He spoke "because he saw" the glory of Jesus. Thus, the problem is not with the Old Testament Scriptures but with the hearts of those who read it.

The Scriptures of the Old Testament, on their own terms, and quite apart from the New Testament interpretation of them, reveal the gospel of Jesus Christ in promise form in a way that can be understood as a function of the perspicuity of the Old Testament itself.

Fifth, and speaking in a much broader covenant-historical frame of reference, Ennsian or Historicist Christotelism loses sight of the basic concern of biblical revelation. God, in his self-revelation, seeks to confer Himself in a covenantal bond of communion on a holy people, in a holy realm, advancing them beyond probation to eternal life and sab-bath rest through the meritorious obedience of a federal head.

The first Adam was to guard the Edenic temple-garden (Gen 2:15), exercise dominion over the Serpent-Dragon by bruising his head (Gen 1:26–28; 2:15–16; 3:1), and, upon successful completion of his pro-bation, take and eat from the tree of life (Gen 3:23–24). Through the perfect and personal obedience of Adam as a federal head, God would advance Adam, and in him his posterity, to a confirmed estate of glory, life, and rest.

What was not accomplished through the first Adam, due to sin, was accomplished by the Last Adam through perfect, personal, exact and en-tire obedience. Jesus Christ, as the Second and Last Adam (1 Cor 15:45, 47) destroys the work of the devil (Gen 3:15; Luke 4:1–13; 23:35–39), covers over the sin of his people and confers His image upon them (Gen 3:21; Lev 1:4, 16; Heb 9:26; Eph 4:24; Col 3:10; Rom 13:14; 1 Cor 15:49, 52–53), bears the wrath and curse of God as a substitute and grants resurrection life as the firstborn from among the dead and head of the church (Gen 3:23–24; John 12:25–26; 1 Cor 15:45; 2 Cor 3:17; Col 1:18; Rev 2:7; 22:1–5, 13–14). All of this is applied to the church by Spirit-wrought union with Christ through faith (Eph 1:13; 2:8–10; 3:16–17).

Enns, in a 2012 volume entitled, *The Evolution of Adam: What the*

Bible Does and Doesn't Say about Human Origins,[15] employs the Christotelic method to deny the existence of the historical Adam as presented
by Paul in 1 Cor 15:45 and Rom 5:12–19. He contends that the Old
Testament presents Adam as a narrative construction who secures the
self-definition of a post-Exilic community—a view common among
theological liberals and critical scholarship.[16] Adam is proto-Israel, not
the first created image-bearing federal head of the human race.[17] Regardless of how deficient Enns' view of Adam in the Old Testament
may be (and it is entirely deficient), what is important to note is that
Enns makes explicit that the same christotelic hermeneutic outlined
above supplies the rationale for charging Paul with error in regard to his
mistaken belief in an historical Adam. He says,

> The reason behind Paul's distinct portrayal of Adam reflects his
> Christ-centered handling of the Old Testament in general, as we saw
> in the previous chapter. Israel's story, including Adam, is now to be
> read in the light of its climax in the death and resurrection of Christ.
> In other words, Paul's understanding of Adam is shaped by Jesus, *not
> the other way around.*[18]

However, Enns has something that most Christians would find highly
unsettling, even shocking. Regarding the Apostle Paul's understanding
of Adam in Rom 5 and 1 Cor 15, he says,

> At the outset we should admit that Adam is a vital theological and
> *historical* figure for Paul. Without question, Adam plays a significant
> theological role for Paul. But Adam's theological significance cannot
> be distanced from Paul's assumption that Adam was the first man
> created by God. . . . Adam's theological importance does not exist for
> Paul independent of Adam's historical position as the first man, from
> whom the human race descended and from whom all inherited sin
> and death. . . . It is Adam as the first man that makes him such a vital
> theological significance.[19]

And getting down to the core of his argument, Enns observes,

> The scientific evidence we have for human origins and the literary

---

15. Peter Enns, *The Evolution of Adam: What the Bible Does and Doesn't Say about
Human Origins* (Grand Rapids, Mich.: Brazos Press, 2012).

16. Ibid., 26–34.

17. Ibid., 141–143.

18. Ibid., 122 (emphasis added).

19. Ibid., 120 (emphasis original).

evidence we have for human origins are so overwhelmingly persuasive that belief in a first human, such as Paul understood him, is not a viable option. The way forward, I believe, is to recognize the profound historical (not simply symbolic) truths in Paul's words that remain *despite his view of human origins.*[20]

Thus, since Enns is explicit that evolution demands that Paul's view of Adam be wrong, and since Paul's imaginative reinterpretation of an historical Adam is set disjunctively over against the Old Testament view of Adam as proto-Israel, Enns opts for the Old Testament view of Adam *instead of Paul's.* He can do this only because he uses the Christotelic method that sets the original "grammatical-historical" understanding of Adam (the first read) over against the "Christotelic" understanding of Adam (the second read), and rejects the Christotelic reading due to the hegemony he grants to evolutionary theory (and not biblical revelation).

In essence, Enns argues that the Apostle Paul is wrong, due in large part to his over-active apostolic imagination that caused him to make errant inferences from the resurrection of Christ. Enns' historicist conception of Christotelism, the reductionistic understanding of grammatical-historical meaning in the "first reading" of the Old Testament, the irreconcilable doctrines of Adam in the Old and New Testaments, and his full commitment to secular evolutionism (e.g., his fundamentalistic and optimistic allegiance to the Genome Project) converge to assist him in charging Paul with error. Enns' Christotelic proposal begins and ends in the quagmire of historicism, rooted in anti-supernatural presuppositions that eviscerate the notion that the Bible is the inerrant Word of God in written form.

Conclusion

Historicist Christotelism turns out to be about the history of religion, or the history of religious experience, rather than the history of special revelation. As such, the roots of Historicist Christotelism are in theological liberalism and the view that the Bible is a fallible record of religious experience. Supernaturalist (or Reformed) Christotelism is instead a history of special revelation, or a history of the progressive and

---

20. Ibid., 122 (emphasis added).

organic unfolding of revelation that has Christ as its central redemptive subject matter and consummate *telos*. Its roots are in the Reformation, Protestant Scholasticism, and their development associated with Old Princeton and Old Amsterdam.

At stake in the debate is whether the church receives the Christ who is truly revealed in the Scriptures of the Old and New Testaments by the supernatural agency of the Spirit, or whether we are to receive the imaginative construal of the religious experience of ancient Hebrews or Second Temple Jews. The former is the produce of the Spirit speaking in Scripture as a revelational record of the history of special revelation; the latter is the produce of the autonomous Kantian ego operating on the phenomena of human experience as community autobiography.

I conclude with a summarizing comment from Richard Gaffin in his response to Clair Davis:

> As Vos indicates . . . at stake here is what is essential for the Reformed faith (e.g., WCF, 7:5–6; 8:6; 11:6; WLC, 33–35), for true, Biblical religion since the fall: the unity of the religion of the Old and New Testaments focused on Christ. Central for the faith of the former is the future fulfillment of the promise of the Messiah to come, for the faith of the latter, the realized fulfillment of that promise . . . Biblical theology undertaken as [Historicist or Ennsian] Christotelic interpretation, no doubt despite the best intentions of many of its practitioners' intentions, which I commend and honor, nonetheless regrettably obscures and compromises that truth.[21]

Related Episodes

- Redemptive-Historical Hermeneutics, Divine Authorship, and the Christotelism Debate
  » http://reformedforum.org/rf14_01
- Redemptive-Historical Hermeneutics, Divine Authorship, and the Christotelism Debate
  » http://reformedforum.org/ctc355
- Redemptive-Historical Hermeneutics with Lane Tipton
  » http://reformedforum.org/ctc186
- Seeing Jesus in Old Testament History with Nancy Guthrie
  » http://reformedforum.org/ctc296

---

21. Gaffin, Jr., "Response to Clair Davis."

- Christ in the Old Testament with Nancy Guthrie
  » http://reformedforum.org/ctc224
- Seeing Jesus in the Old Testament with Nancy Guthrie
  » http://reformedforum.org/ctc183
- Seeing Jesus in the Prophets with Nancy Guthrie
  » http://reformedforum.org/ctc340
- Sacrifices and Festivals in the Old Testament with Ben Shaw
  » http://reformedforum.org/ctc95
- Jesus on Every Page with David Murray
  » http://reformedforum.org/ctc299
- Seeing Christ in All of Scripture with Vern Poythress and Iain Duguid
  » http://reformedforum.org/ctc439
- Ephesians 6:10–17 and a Biblical Theology of Clothing with Will Wood
  » http://reformedforum.org/ctc431
- Typology and Jehoiachin with Matthew Patton
  » http://reformedforum.org/ctc284
- Walking with Jesus Through His Word with Dennis Johnson
  » http://reformedforum.org/ctc453
- Symbols and Types
  » http://reformedforum.org/ctc471

4

BIBLICAL AND SYSTEMATIC THEOLOGY

CAMDEN M. BUCEY

G OD IS NOT silent. He has spoken and continues to speak definitively and emphatically by His Spirit through His Word. In speaking that Word, God has related to us in a way we can understand. For Christians who have studied God's Word for years this may come as obvious, but we ought not take this for granted. Westminster Confession of Faith 7.1 reminds us of our relationship to God,

> The distance between God and the creature is so great, that although reasonable creatures do owe obedience unto him as their Creator, yet they could never have any fruition of him as their blessedness and reward, but by some voluntary condescension on God's part, which he hath been pleased to express by way of covenant.

Apart from God's covenantal condescension unto us, we would never know him as our blessedness and reward. We would comprehend nothing of him apart from his revelation. God is transcendent and we cannot comprehend him. The prophet Isaiah reveals this very truth, "'For my thoughts are not your thoughts, neither are your ways my ways,' declares the LORD. 'For as the heavens are higher than the earth, so are my ways higher than your ways and my thoughts than your thoughts'"

(Isa 55:8–9). But the Lord has not seen fit to leave us in a state of igno-
rance. He has indeed come down to us.

Everything we know is a result of revelation. He does not learn
things, but is the eternal and omniscient source of all truth. God is the
original knower, who serves as the foundation and ultimate reference
point of all knowledge. We come to know things truly, but always
revelationally and analogously to the way in which God knows.

Forms of Revelation

God has revealed himself first in the things that have been made. We
call this general revelation. The psalmist exclaims, "The heavens declare the glory of God, and the sky above proclaims his handiwork"
(Ps 19:1). Paul wrote declared that God's, "invisible attributes, namely,
his eternal power and divine nature, have been clearly perceived, ever
since the creation of the world, in the things that have been made"
(Rom 1:20). This knowledge of God is ineradicable. His divine finger-
prints are on everything. The great Swiss reformer John Calvin taught
that knowledge of God is implanted within humanity, and therefore
to know oneself truly is simultaneously to know God. We are indeed
created in his image (Gen 1:27).

Second, God has revealed himself through his Word in dreams, vi-
sions, speech, and Scripture. We call this form special revelation. While
God revealed himself ecstatically to the prophets and apostles, we believe that form of revelation has ceased with the closing of the canon of
Scripture. Since the foundation has now been laid, there is no further
need to lay another (Eph 2:20). This is not to say that God is presently
silent or that we are lacking his communication in this present age,
"For the word of God is living and active, sharper than any two-edged
sword, piercing to the division of soul and of spirit, of joints and of
marrow, and discerning the thoughts and intentions of the heart" (Heb
4:12). God has spoken and continues to speak, though now he speaks
by the Holy Spirit through Scripture. "All Scripture is breathed out by
God and profitable for teaching, for reproof, for correction, and for
training in righteousness" (2 Tim 3:16). The breathed-out character of
God's word is its *inspiration*. Peter writes that, "no prophecy of Scripture comes from someone's own interpretation. For no prophecy was
ever produced by the will of man, but men spoke from God as they

were carried along by the Holy Spirit" (2 Pet 1:20–21). The Holy Spirit worked in human writers to record his Word. To employ Peter's metaphor, he was the wind in their sails. The human instruments are the secondary authors; God is the primary. God used the personalities, life experiences, and unique characteristics of each human author such that every word, sentence, paragraph, and book is his very Word. But we can say so much more, since God has inspired Scripture. Among other things, it is inerrant, infallible, authoritative, necessary, sufficient, and perspicuous. God cannot make mistakes; he cannot lie; he cannot fail in communicating himself clearly to us; and he certainly never has a problem getting his message across.

These divisions of general and special revelation are not the sum total of God's revelation to humanity. The Triune God has revealed himself climactically in his Son.

> Long ago, at many times and in many ways, God spoke to our fathers by the prophets, but in these last days he has spoken to us by his Son, whom he appointed the heir of all things, through whom also he created the world. He is the radiance of the glory of God and the exact imprint of his nature, and he upholds the universe by the word of his power (Heb 1:1–3a).

God has spoken to us in a new way, which is not to say that God's revelation was somehow insufficient before the coming of our Lord Jesus Christ. The revelation is substantially the same, but it now has come with greater brightness. Before, it was given in types and shadows. Now it shines in the face of the resurrected Son. Consider the effect of a magnifying glass. It does not alter the power of the sun's light, yet it collects the disparate individual rays of light into a concentrated beam. Likewise, the various threads of covenant history find their purpose and climax in Jesus Christ. Particularly in his resurrection, the light of Christ shines forth with a greater and more concentrated force than ever before. The substance of God's light has not changed; yet it has now been brought to bear in his glorious Son.

Studying Theology

Because God's revelation is the foundation for all our knowledge of God, we must also recognize that the various theological disciplines relate to one another. The great Reformed apologist Cornelius Van Til

(1895–1987) emphasized this fact as he described the theological encyclopedia. This is a technical way to speak about all the disciplines of theology. These are the various segments of study which typically define the departments of a seminary or other religious school. We cannot consider them independent silos of knowledge. Rather, the subject matters interrelate and inform one another deeply. Each discipline is one facet of a glorious jewel of the knowledge of God.

Biblical studies, perhaps the most foundational of theological disciplines, is itself usually divided between Old and New Testaments. It also takes up the study of hermeneutics (the science of interpretation). Church history or historical studies examines the events, persons, ideas, movements, and consequent lessons of the past. Apologetics focuses on the defense of the faith and its related philosophical matters. Practical theology is perhaps the most varied of the bunch. It often focuses on the application of theological truth to specific activities in the Christian life, such as preaching, worship, and counseling. Systematic theology seeks to organize the whole of God's revelation into topics. In his book, *Biblical Theology: Old and New Testaments*,[1] Geerhardus Vos describes this topical arrangement as drawing a circle.

Systematic theology is concerned with asking the following: What does the Bible *as a whole* teach about any specific subject? In other words, systematic theology seeks to organize the content of revelation topically. Traditionally, theologians have grouped these topics into several large divisions, called the theological *loci*.[2] These are the big headings under which all systematic studies fall. Prolegomena explores foundational issues, such as God's revelation and the doctrine of Scripture. Theology proper is the study of God's being and attributes. Anthropology is the study of humanity. Christology studies the person and work of our redeemer, Jesus Christ. Pneumatology examines the work of the Holy Spirit in applying Christ's life, death, and resurrection to his people. Ecclesiology focuses on the doctrine of the church. Eschatology is the study of last things. Others studies are occasionally mentioned, such

---

1. Geerhardus Vos, *Biblical Theology: Old and New Testaments* (Grand Rapids, Mich.: Wm. B. Eerdmans Publishing Company, 1948; revised ed. Banner of Truth Trust, 1975).

2. "Loci" is a Latin word. It is the plural form of locus, which means "center" or "source."

as hamartology (the doctrine of sin) or sacramentology (the doctrine of the sacraments), yet these are frequently subsumed under the broader, traditional *loci*.

Systematic theology itself assumes different flavors. It can be programmatic or polemical—seeking to blaze a trail by advancing a topic or criticizing another existing view. Yet even within these modes of theologizing, different nuances emerge. Many systematicians emphasize historical theology, while others gravitate toward philosophy. Regardless of one's proclivities, all true systematicians ought to engage in exegesis. Whether systematic, historical, or practical, all theology must be a product of exegesis. We propose a radically non-speculative theology. That is, our theologizing is not imaginative. We are not creating things, properly speaking, but seeking to understand and organize what God has revealed to us. Faithful theology is receptively reconstructive of God's revealed thoughts.

There is a related discipline, which rarely ever receives its own department. It is known as "biblical theology"—a most curious name, since all theology should be "biblical." Geerhardus Vos (1862–1949) is recognized as the father of Reformed biblical theology. He preferred the title, "the history of special revelation," because it underscored the progressive and unfolding nature of God's covenantal communication to mankind. But by the time Vos provided his input, the academy had already settled on nomenclature. Despite the name, Vos never ceased his efforts to bring the new discipline into conformity to God's Word. Vos was the first professor to occupy the chair of biblical theology at Princeton Theological Seminary. He battled the influence classic liberalism and modern biblical criticism advanced by Johann Eichhorn (1752–1827) and further developed by Julius Wellhausen (1844–1918). Johann Gabler (1753–1826) is perhaps most directly responsible for weaving this modernist thread into the nascent discipline of biblical theology. Vos was singularly equipped to meet this challenge, yet outside conservative Reformed circles he is all but unknown.

The Relationship between Biblical and Systematic Theology

Gabler believed biblical theology was purely descriptive of the beliefs of the biblical authors. As a discipline, it should be distinguished sharply from dogmatic or systematic theology, which he believed ought to be a contextualized application of biblical theology's findings. This approach is deeply problematic. Biblical and systematic theology should not be considered independently. These disciplines mutually regulate and inform each other. Let us consider the consequences of rejecting such a relationship.

If systematic theology were to operate independently, what tendencies might it exhibit? One danger is that of abstraction. If we seek to organize the content of Scripture topically with no regard to the particular setting of Scripture, we may end up with a bare abstract conclusion that has little or nothing to do with actual covenant history. Systematic theology must always be anchored by the concrete redemptive-historical context of Scripture. Scripture exists as an unbreakable unity, which forms the foundation requisite for systematic theology. If Scripture were not united, then we would have no proper basis to rest our abstractions and topical analyses. Any relation would rest upon the mind of the theologian, not upon anything objective or inherent in the text itself and the history it records.

Scripture cannot be treated as an uninterpreted collection of discreet data. It is organic and progressively unfolding. It is an inspired, inerrant, infallible record of God's covenant communication. It is dynamic, and we cannot treat it as a static collection of truth independent of the times and places in which it was revealed. If God desired to drop a completed canon out of the sky, he would have done so. Instead, God chose to speak to his people in varied ages and places as a means of nurturing his covenant communion bond. He entered into a living relationship with them. Treating Scripture exclusively as a static whole would be to neglect this essential aspect of its character, and therefore it is important to take methodological steps to prevent such mishandling. We can prevent the error of bare abstraction by appealing to biblical theology. Whereas systematic theology seeks to organize the Bible topically and logically by drawing a circle, biblical theology seeks to represent the progressive unfolding of revelation in history by drawing a line. In brief, the difference between biblical and systematic theology is the difference between historical and logical construction.

To describe the history of special revelation, Vos used the metaphor of a seed. As it is nourished, it buds and begins to blossom into a beautifully developed flower. The principle and promise of the flower is there all along; it is *organic* to the process. It is the natural and intended result inherent within the seed. Revelation is likewise organic as God reveals himself to humanity progressively. Revelation is given first in seed form, but throughout covenant history, it buds and blossoms unto the full flower of the resurrected savior Jesus Christ. While the *line* was being drawn, *circles* were being drawn as well. Vos writes, "It should be remembered that on the line of historical progress there is at several points already a *beginning of correlation* among elements of truth in which *the beginnings of the systematizing process can be discerned.*"[3] This means that systematic theology is not a discipline alien to biblical theology. Whereas Gabler regarded systematic theology as an imposition upon Scripture, we recognize that even within God's unfolding revelation, the seeds of systematization have been sown and have begun to blossom.

We have already addressed the danger of abstracting the content of Scripture without reference to the concrete particulars of redemptive history. This is one way that biblical theology can regulate systematic theology. Another danger would be to concentrate on the individual concrete events of covenant history without respect to the whole. This is an atomistic approach to Scripture in which every occasion is unrelated to the others. You cannot read Scripture faithfully while wearing such blinders. This is one way that systematic theology can regulate biblical theology. As a discipline, systematic theology helps us to see how the events of covenant history relate to one another. We may compare earlier revelation with later revelation—to interpret Scripture with Scripture. Systematic and biblical theology are not antagonistic. Both rely upon exegetical theology, and they mutually contextualize, regulate, and inform each other. Systematic theology should never be engaged apart from biblical theology, and *vice versa*.

At Reformed Forum, we believe this distinctive method is neither tangential nor arbitrary. It is a direct and essential consequence of the nature of God's revelation. We simply do not have the choice to engage in theological study any other way. But when we engage God's revelation in the way he intended, we gain a greater appreciation for the beauty and grandeur of our Triune God's communication. He has revealed himself through covenant history and has unfolded his plan to

---

3. Geerhardus Vos, *Biblical Theology: Old and New Testaments* (Banner of Truth, 1975), 16 (emphasis added).

bring glory unto himself through the person and work of His Son, our savior, Jesus Christ.

Related Episodes

- The Nature and Method of Biblical Theology, Part 1
  » http://reformedforum.org/ctc315
- The Nature and Method of Biblical Theology, Part 2
  » http://reformedforum.org/ctc320
- Systematic Theology: An Introduction to Christian Belief with John Frame
  » http://reformedforum.org/ctc312
- Biblical Theology and the Westminster Standards
  » http://reformedforum.org/ctc6
- Nature and Scripture with K. Scott Oliphint
  » http://reformedforum.org/ctc240
- Van Til's Trinitarian Theology with Lane Tipton
  » http://reformedforum.org/ctc49
- God's Mighty Acts in the Old Testament with Richard C. Gamble
  » http://reformedforum.org/ctc77
- The Final Word: Christ the Son in Hebrews 1:1–4, Lane Tipton
  » http://reformedforum.org/rf14_13
- The Theological Interpretation of Scripture with Nathaniel Gray Sutanto
  » http://reformedforum.org/ctc473
- God… With Us with K. Scott Oliphint
  » http://reformedforum.org/ctc205

5

Union with Christ
and the *Ordo Salutis*

Jeffrey C. Waddington

A seminary professor friend of mine says that union with Christ is the "central soteric blessing." I think he is right. What does that even mean? It will be the goal of this chapter to unpack the meaning and significance of union with Christ, and by the time we reach our conclusion, I hope to have convinced you that my friend is right. First we will look at the broad sweep of biblical evidence for the believer's union with Jesus. Second we will drill down deep in Rom 5:12–21 to consider the covenantal structure of our union with the first and second Adams. Third we will ponder the significance of union with Christ in some figures in church history. Fourth we will examine the contemporary discussion of union within conservative Reformed circles. Finally, we will briefly conclude with some thoughts on the practical effects of this teaching. Before we dig into this rich soil of Rom 5:12–21, it would be well to look at the big picture of the doctrine of union with Christ.

The Biblical Panorama of Union

Union with Christ is inextricably intertwined with federal headship. The Bible actually teaches that every last individual save Jesus is born under the federal headship of Adam (Gen 1–3, Rom 5:12–21). We are all naturally "in Adam." To be "in Adam" is to be united to him. Adam is not just the father of the whole human race. He is also the public representative of the whole human race. When Adam fell he took us all down with him. The quip is quite right, "In Adam's fall, we sinned all!" What Adam did is *debited* to our account. There are three ways (at least) that we can understand this fallout: it led to our guilt, our corruption, and our alienation. We are guilty of Adam's first transgression by virtue of Adam's federal headship. We have forfeited our original righteousness, holiness, and knowledge. And we have become alienated from a holy God and from one another and from our environment. We are united to Adam and suffer the severe consequences of his one act of disobedience whether we like it or not. Frankly, given the spiritually dead condition we inherit we are not likely to object to this state of affairs beyond thinking it highly unfair. As Paul tells us in Eph 2:3, though, we *are* "children of wrath."

God's answer to the fall and our union with Adam is the sending of his Son in the flesh (John 1:14). Jesus Christ, the Son of God joined to a human nature (a "true body" and a "reasonable soul" as the WSC Q&A 22 has it), came to undo the results of the fall. The big difference between the fall and our being in Adam and redemption and our being "in Christ" is that with Adam we are all in him by birth. Union with Christ is by faith in Jesus who is presented to us in the gospel. That is, we hear the gospel and respond to God's rich mercy and grace towards us. When the Holy Spirit works in us to enable us to see Christ in all his beauty and strength and holiness and righteousness, and we understand that the holy life he lived and the death he died and the resurrection he underwent, he did *for us* and consequently believe on him as Savior and Lord, we are then joined to Christ in a way analogous to our union with Adam. Once we are in Christ we are no longer in Adam. We have *transferred* from the kingdom of darkness to the kingdom of God's beloved Son (Col 1:13). This union with Christ manifests what are called benefits or blessings. These blessings answer to and indeed surpass the fallout from Adam's first transgression; justification answers the problem of our guilt before a holy God. Definitive (as well as positional and progressive) sanctification addresses our loss of holiness and the corruption of our whole nature. Adoption deals with our alienation. Glorification as bodily resurrection, while not "in this life," is the culmination of our sanctification in this life. As the Westminster Divines point out in the Shorter Catechism, these main benefits are accompanied by others such as joy in the Holy Spirit, peace of conscience, increase of grace (that is, our increasing ability to daily die to sin and live to righteousness), and perseverance of our Christian walk unto the end of our life (WSC Q&A 36).

In a nutshell, our union with Jesus Christ by a faith worked out in us by the internal working of God the Holy Spirit connects us to our living and reigning Savior and Lord so that what is true of him as the God-man and as our Mediator is also true of us. In his righteous life Jesus was living obediently to God the Father and that obedience to God's will is *credited* to our account (often referred to as "imputation"). Jesus' death under God's curse is something he did *for us* and *in our place*. Jesus took upon himself the just judgment and punishment which all those who have been chosen before the foundation of the world (Eph 1:3) and have believed on Jesus otherwise deserved. Jesus' resurrection was God's removal of the curse that fell on Jesus for bearing our sin (Gal 3:13) and it is the Father's stamp of approval on his Son's work for us. In other words, the resurrection was Christ's justification (1 Tim 3:16). It was also his definitive sanctification in that the resurrection represented the absolute break of the stranglehold of Satan and sin on Christ (Rom 6:1–14). Christ's resurrection was also his coronation as the Son of God-in-power (Rom 1:1–5) as he entered into his estate of exaltation after having lived in an estate of humiliation for some thirty-three years. In the world of that time a kingly coronation would be spoken of in terms of adoption so we can think of Jesus' resurrection as his adoption (this is not to be confused with the error of *adoptionism* which is something altogether different).

Union with Christ is the gracious divine means of reversing the effects of the Adamic fall. Union with Christ is, to use the thought of erstwhile Westminster Seminary professor John Murray, the "umbrella" that embraces all the facets of the application of redemption.[1]

Drilling Down Deep into the
Romans 5 Basis of Union with Christ

We have spied out a bird's eye view of the biblical foundations for a doctrine of union with Christ. Now we turn to dig deeper into Rom 5:12–21.[2] This is not the only place in the Bible where we can find rich resources from which to construct a doctrine of union with Jesus Christ. It is not even the only place in Romans. Romans 6, for instance, continues consideration of our union with the Lord in his death, burial, and resurrection and the implications of these events for our definitive sanctification.

The apostle Paul evinces the eschatalogically-charged covenantal structure of the accomplishment and application of redemption in Rom 5:12–21. Specifically, Paul has in view the dual headship of Adam and Christ and our relationship to both. Romans 5 provides a hinge between Paul's consideration of justification and sanctification. Paul has addressed the universal problem of sin from Rom 1:18–3:20. From Rom 3:21–5:11 the apostle is concerned with how God addresses the particular problem of the guilt of sin in the blessing of justification. Rom 6:1–8:39 speaks to the problem of the corruption, power, or pollution of sin and how God addresses it with the blessing of definitive sanctification.

Romans 5:12–21 opens up for us a window on the architectonic structure of the two federal heads: Adam and Jesus Christ. Death has come upon all men through the sin of the one man Adam. Life has come to all through the one act of Christ's righteousness. Implicit in Paul's consideration of the two federal heads is the eschatalogically-infused covenantal character of God's dealings with the human race in the covenant of works and the covenant of grace. One may wonder why Adam's finite, temporal act of disobedience would warrant eternal

---

1. John Murray, *Redemption Accomplished and Applied* (Grand Rapids, Mich.: Eerdmans, 2015). Murray's point is that union with Christ is not one benefit among others but is the context in which all the benefits of the "ordo salutis" or application of redemption come to us.

2. We will not delve into Paul's discussion of the Law in Rom 5:12–21. While it is germane to a fuller consideration of union, it is outside the purview of this chapter.

death. One could just as easily ask how Christ's finite, temporal act of obedience warrants eternal life.[3]

God's act of creation and his interaction with Adam were covenantal. In other words, God was under no obligation to act beneficially towards Adam and Eve. God voluntarily condescended to create and enter into fellowship with Adam and then even more so later to redeem a fallen people. God set forth deep and rich fellowship with him as a reward for obedience to his command to refrain from eating from the tree of the knowledge of good and evil. Implicit in the warning about imminent death was great blessing for obedience. Lane Tipton speaks of this covenantal bond of communion as "sacramental" in nature.[4] Adam could have had uninterrupted blissful communion with the Triune God had he listened and heeded the direction of the Lord in the garden. Subsequent to the fall, it would take faith in Jesus Christ, the incarnate God-man, to reach the estate of uninterrupted blessing of rich fellowship with God. This is what it means to say that the architectonic structure of creation, providence, and redemption is *eschatalogically-charged covenantalism.*

Getting back to the immediate context of Rom 5:12–21, Paul does not mean to suggest that *all* men benefit from the one act of Christ's obedience *simpliciter*. The relationship between Adam and Christ is *not*, in this case, exactly symmetrical. All men, women, boys, and girls are brought down by Adam's treachery. We all, by virtue of being born into this world, are sons and daughters of Adam and therefore are infected with sin's guilt, corruption, and alienation. We could say that we are born in sin by virtue of being fallen human beings. But being born human is not sufficient for being "in Christ." One must savingly believe on Jesus to be united to him. That is, one must exercise faith towards the Jesus of the Bible and this involves a *subset* or fraction of the whole human race.[5] The set of all those born in Adam and therefore born in

---

3. I am not taking into consideration Christ's ultimately supreme inherent value as our Redeemer. If we were to explore that question, the previous concern would evaporate.

4. From unpublished lectures given in the "Van Til's Trinitarian Theology" PhD seminar at Westminster Theological Seminary in Glenside, PA. Fall 2016 semester.

5. I am purposefully distancing orthodox Reformed doctrine and life from the influence of Swiss theologian Karl Barth and those who follow him such as the late Thomas F. Torrance.

sin is universal. The set of those who believe on Jesus Christ unto salvation is partial, not universal.

When Paul notes that "because all sinned" he does not indicate *merely* that we all imitate or follow the example of Adam any more than that we are saved by imitating the one righteous act of Jesus.[6] When Adam sinned he acted *in the place of* and *on behalf of* or *for* those he represented. That is, for all men since he was the federal head for the whole human race. In a like manner, what Christ did (thinking here of his *one act* of obedience unto death as the culmination of a whole life of obedience to God's law) he did for his people.

It is also worth noticing that Paul is comparing and contrasting the *one man* Adam and his *one act* of disobedience to the *one man* Jesus Christ and his *one act* of righteousness. In the case of Adam at least, we are concerned with his disobedience to the prohibition and not with all the other sins that followed. In neither case is Paul not simply concerned with external actions but with external actions that manifest internal dispositions or states of the heart. Paul is not concerned with either the external eating of forbidden fruit alone on the one hand, or the bloody death of a crucifixion on the other. Paul is concerned with what led to the one act of disobedience or the one act of obedience. In the case of Adam, he desired to be wise by a path forbidden by God. In the case of Christ, the second Adam, he desired to be obedient according to the terms set by the Father. It is the state of the heart that mastication manifested and what submission to a life of pain and misery culminating in the "utterly vile death of the cross"[7] indicated that is also in view insofar as these bear on the covenantal and federal nature of the impetration and application of redemption.

All this semi-technical discussion is meant to illustrate the shape of our union with Adam in sin and our union with Christ by grace through faith. Union with Christ is one strand of the whole cloth of federalism or covenant theology. To properly understand what union with Christ means we need to rightly appreciate the larger structure within which it functions: the dual public representative roles of Adam and Christ. Christ not only comes to undo the damage done by Adam thought of in negative terms but Christ also comes to provide for us

---

6. I take the prepositional phrase ἐφ' ᾧ πάντες ἥμαρτον to mean "in that all sinned."
7. Or *mors turpissima crucis*, from the early church father Origen of Alexandria.

what we missed out on in Adam. This gets at what is typically referred to as the eschatological color of redemptive history, and we would do well to remind ourselves that we not only lost something in the fall but also fell short of the promised blessing of communal fellowship with the Triune God.

Historical Examples of How Union with Christ Has Been Understood

The doctrine of union with Christ is a fairly common theological trope in the history of the church so it would be an unwieldy exercise to try to give even a cursory review of what every major theologian thought about the doctrine. While that would be a worthwhile endeavor, my concern in this section is to offer brief consideration of some significant Reformed theologians, namely, John Calvin, Walter Marshall, Jonathan Edwards, and the divines of the Westminster Assembly. This is merely meant to be a suggestive list. Calvin deals with the doctrine of union in his justly famous *Institutes of the Christian Religion*. Walter Marshall delineates his understanding of union in his *Gospel Mystery of Sanctification*. Jonathan Edwards deals with union throughout his variegated and voluminous literary corpus, but our focus shall fall on his *Discourse on Justification*. Finally, we will examine what the Westminster divines formulated in the *Larger Catechism*.[8]

As with our other theologians under consideration here, John Calvin's (1509–1564) ruminations on union with Christ are not limited to his *Institutes*.[9] As with Edwards, we possess a wealth of Calvin resources in his sermons, personal correspondence, biblical commentaries, monographs, as well as the *Institutes*. We are focusing on the *Institutes* for space and simplicity's sake. Calvin was preceded in his consideration of

---

8. I recognize that the Larger Catechism represents an official doctrinal standard in historically Presbyterian denominations so that it is unique among the documents and theologians looked at here. This distinction also accounts for the Westminster Assembly bring treated out of chronological sequence.

9. John Calvin, *Institutes of the Christian Religion* (Ford Lewis Battles, tr. John T. McNeill, ed. Louisville,KY, Westminster John Knox Press, 1961), 2 vols. There are several versions of the Institutes available in English including the Beveridge and Allen editions as well as fresh English translations of earlier editions of the *Institutes* than the final Latin edition of 1559. Most recently two translations of one of the French versions of the *Institutes* provide us with fresh insight.

union with Christ in the theologies of, among others, Bernard of Clair-veaux and Martin Luther. In other words, Calvin learned the doctrine from Scripture and other theologians who meditated on the spiritual richness of union because it was found in Scripture.

In the *Institutes* Calvin develops what he refers to as the twofold blessing of God (*"duplex gratia Dei"*) that arises out of the believer's union with Jesus Christ. According to Calvin, what Christ has done for his people in the history of redemption is of no value as long as they remain outside of Christ and at a distance from him.

> How do we receive those benefits which the Father bestowed on his only-begotten Son—not for Christ's own private use, but that he might enrich poor and needy men? First, we must understand that as long as Christ remains outside of us, and we are separated from him, all that he has suffered and done for the salvation of the human race remains useless and of no value for us. Therefore, to share with us what he has received from the Father, he had to become ours and to dwell within us. For this reason, he is called "our Head" [Eph. 4:15], and "the first-born among many brethren" [Rom. 8:29]. We also, in turn, are said to be "engrafted into him" [Rom. 11:17], and to "put on Christ" [Gal. 3:27]; for, as I have said, all that he possesses is nothing to us until we grow into one body with him. It is true that we obtain this by faith.[10]

For the believer to benefit from Christ's holy life, sacrificial death, res-urrection, ascension, and heavenly session, he or she must be united to Christ by the bond of faith created by the internal, subjective work of the Holy Spirit. It is the context of union with Christ that brings about the believer's justification, adoption, and definitive sanctification.[11]

Calvin uses the expression "twofold blessing" with reference specifi-cally to justification and sanctification or regeneration.[12] Calvin writes at a time before the more precise language distinguishing different as-

---

10. Calvin, *Institutes*, III.i.1 (1:537).

11. Calvin does not use the language of definitive sanctification. This expression was first coined by John Murray. However, the expression captures the reality Calvin is addressing here.

12. Calvin, *Institutes*, II.xvi.6 (1:512) and elsewhere. "Therefore, in Christ's death and burial a twofold blessing is set forth for us to enjoy: liberation from the death to which we had been bound, and mortification of our flesh." In this first reference Calvin is speaking about Christ's death and resurrection, but these are the redemptive-histori-cal bases for justification and sanctification.

pects of the internal, subjective work of the Holy Spirit in the life of the believer are more fully delineated. Sanctification and regeneration possess semantic overlap so that either word may refer to the initial new birth, the dramatic breach with sin, or the ongoing, lifelong maturation in grace that we typically associate with progressive sanctification. It seems clear that justification and sanctification come together in union. One redemptive benefit is not the foundation or basis for the other. The basis of each is the person and work of Jesus Christ. Calvin draws upon the logic of the Chalcedonian formula to provide shape to his understanding of the relationship of justification and sanctification. This twofold blessing forms a package in which justification and sanctification are "distinct, yet inseparable." To be justified without also being sanctified is to "tear Christ" into "pieces."

> But, since the question concerns only righteousness and sanctification, let us dwell upon these. Although we may distinguish them, Christ contains both of them inseparably in himself. Do you wish, then, to attain righteousness in Christ? You must first possess Christ; but you cannot possess him without being made partaker in his sanctification, because he cannot be divided into pieces [1 Cor. 1:13]. Since, therefore, it is solely by expending himself that the Lord gives us these benefits to enjoy, he bestows both of them at the same time, the one never without the other. Thus it is clear how true it is that we are justified not without works yet not through works, since in our sharing in Christ, which justifies us, sanctification is just as much included as righteousness.[13]

One could say that the relation works in either direction since the two benefits are clearly distinguished and yet both are grounded in the Lord Jesus Christ to whom the believer is united.

While Calvin differs from the Lutheran tradition in understanding the relation of justification to union with Christ, he does not fail to maintain doctrinal clarity nor does he forfeit the biblical gains of the Protestant Reformation. Whether Calvin differs significantly from Martin Luther himself, it is clear he differs from later Lutheran dogmatic formulations.[14] Whereas for Calvin union involves the twofold

---

13. Calvin, *Institutes*, III.xvi.1 (1:798).

14. To fully enter into this discussion would take us too far afield. It would require reckoning with recent Luther scholarship and the whole Finnish reading of Luther. We would also have to look at Lutheran dogmatics such as the work of Francis Pieper. New

blessing, in which justification and sanctification come to the believer who is united to Christ, for Lutheranism, justification *is outside of and leads into* union with Christ. In this scenario union appears to be equated with sanctification only. That is certainly how some nineteenth century Lutheran biblical scholars understood union in the writings of Paul.[15]

Perhaps less well-known than Calvin or Edwards, but certainly no less significant for all that, is Walter Marshall's *The Gospel Mystery of Sanctification*.[16] Marshall was a Reformed-oriented non-conformist cleric (1628–1680) in the UK who grew increasingly concerned with the creeping moralism of his day and how a failure to rightly understand justification undermined a proper *understanding of* and *appreciation for* one's sanctification. While one does not find the language of Calvin's twofold blessing in Marshall per se, the theology undergirding his work is clearly akin to Calvin's. While one could not be blamed for thinking Marshall's book is somewhat misnamed. At the end of the day it really isn't.

Walter Marshall sought to unpack the biblical, theological, and experiential benefits of properly understanding union with Christ and the relation of justification and sanctification as the fruit of the believer's union with the Savior in a series of fourteen "directions." He argues throughout the book that the benefits of union with Christ are conveyed to us through the use of the ordinary means of grace: the Word, sacraments, prayer (in the church). The perennial temptation is to *confuse* justification and sanctification or to *blur* the distinction. The error of the medieval Roman Catholic church was attempting to make a reappearance in the English established church in the guise of Laudian latitudinarianism.[17] Not that archbishop Laud was actually a secret Papist. But the Arminianism he represented tended to breed ceremonial-

---

perspective on Paul matters would also enter into the conversation. Then there would be the 19th Lutheran critical biblical scholarship too.

15. Here I have in mind someone like Albert Schweitzer.

16. Walter Marshall, *The Gospel Mystery of Sanctification* (London: 1692). There are at least three versions of this book that I am currently aware of plus electronic forms. One edition is published by Reformation Heritage Books and has a helpful introduction by Joel Beeke. The Wipf & Stock edition has a helpful subtitle that gets at the meat of the nut: "Growing in Holiness by Living in Union with Christ."

17. Named for the archbishop of Canterbury William Laud (1573–1645).

ism and a lurch back towards sacerdotalism. Marshall was concerned to guard the Protestant and Reformed understanding of union with Christ with its proper understanding of justification as a forensic declaration of forgiveness of sin and imputation of Christ's active and passive obedience to the believer. Justification is not about doing just so many good works, nor is it about the internal work of the Holy Spirit. Justification is complete and perfect and our assurance of salvation depends upon an existential awareness of the true nature of justification.

Sanctification is also grounded in our union with Christ and does relate to the internal, subjective work of the Holy Spirit in the life of the believer. Sanctification involves both the decisive breach with sin, being set apart to God in positional sanctification, and the ongoing growth in grace so that the Christian increases in obedience to the Lord by daily putting sin to death and living in righteousness. If we make sanctification the sole basis for our assurance of faith, that assurance will rise and fall like an amusement park roller coaster. While this may be the common lot of many Christians, our assurance should be built on the finished work of Christ and secondarily our obedience can confirm our assurance attained through faith in Christ and his perfect righteousness.[18] Marshall can be tough going for the modern reader, but working through *Gospel Mystery* more than repays the effort.

Jonathan Edwards (1703–1758), the Congregationalist pastor-theologian from Northampton and Stockbridge, is known for his insights into religious psychology and his involvement in and critical support for the First Great Awakening. What may be less well known is that he considered the giving of a series of weekday lectures on justification by faith alone as the divinely used human catalyst of the 1734 revival in Northampton.[19] While Edwards delivered his defense of his Master's question on the Reformed and Protestant doctrine of justification, it is this discourse on justification that will focus our attention.[20]

---

18. The WLC Q&A 80 tells us that there are three legs to the assurance stool: the internal witness of the Holy Spirit, the promises of God in Scripture, and the observation of progress in sanctification.

19. See Jonathan Edwards' preface to his "Five Discourses on Important Subjects," in which he states that the series on justification played a role in the 1734 revival. *The Works of Jonathan Edwards*. 2 vols. (Edward Hickman, ed. Carlisle, PA: Banner of Truth, 1974), 1:620.

20. Jonathan Edwards, *The Works of Jonathan Edwards: Vol. 14/Sermons and Dis-*

Edwards' justification discourse comes in at approximately one-hundred pages in the Yale edition of the work.[21] It seems clear that the published version of the series was beefed up for posterity. In this treatise Edwards addresses the nature of justifying faith (he quibbles with the felicity of the language of faith as the *instrument* of justification),[22] he anticipates and rejects the later New Perspective on Paul idea that works of the Law are works of the ceremonial Law only[23] (i.e., boundary markers such as circumcision, kosher dietary laws, and Sabbath observance), and he ventures the idea of virtual perseverance.[24] Virtual perseverance is the idea that with the first act of faith in Christ and the believer's "unition" with him,[25] included in that act of faith is the virtue of Christ's perseverance to the end/final goal of his life. For our purposes one of the more significant things Edwards says is that justification is *grounded* in the believer's union with Christ.[26] To put this another way, the believer is declared forgiven and righteous in the sight of God because of the holy life, sacrificial death, and resurrection of Christ. In fact, building on the comment by Paul in 1 Tim 3:16 that Christ was "vindicated" by the Spirit, Edwards notes that the believer is justified in Christ because he himself was justified by his resurrection from the dead.[27] The Father through the Spirit lifted the curse which was placed upon Christ in his death (Gal 3:13) by raising him from the dead to newness of life (Rom 6:4).

---

courses, 1723–1729 (Kenneth P. Minkema, ed. New Haven, CT: Yale University Press, 1997), 55–64. This oral defense was read in Latin to the audience at what came to be known as Yale University at Edwards' graduation from his Master of Arts program. This document is referred to as his *QUÆSTIO: PECCATOR NON IUSTIFICATUR CORAM DEO NISI PER IUSTITIAM CHRISTI FIDE APPREHENSAM.*

21. Jonathan Edwards, *The Works of Jonathan Edwards: Vol. 19/Sermons and Discourses, 1734–1738* (M. X. Lesser, ed. New Haven, CT: Yale University Press, 2001), 143–242.

22. Edwards, *WJE*/19:153ff.

23. Edwards, *WJE*/19:147ff.

24. Edwards preached a whole sermon on this as well which can be found in the same volume as the justification discourse, "Persevering Faith," *WJE*/19: 595–608.

25. Language of unition can first be found at *WJEH*/1:626.

26. Edwards, *WJE*/19:154–159ff.

27. Edwards, *WJE*/19: 205 where, commenting on Philippians 3, Edwards notes that the apostle "elsewhere teaches" that our justification is grounded in the justification of Christ which is his resurrection. The verb typically translated as "vindicated" here is ἐδικαιώθη which can properly be translated "justified" by the Spirit.

Finally, we will look at the deliverance of the Westminster Assembly in the *Larger Catechism*. The assembly of divines (i.e., theologians) met from 1643 to 1653 at the invitation of the English parliament in the midst of a civil war between parliament and King Charles I.[28] While there is a fine consistency between the *Confession of Faith*, the *Larger Catechism*, and the *Shorter Catechism*, the centrality of union with Christ *viz-a-viz* the benefits of redemption, is most clearly spelled out in the WLC. We should remember that unlike the theologians we have looked at thus far in this historical survey, the WLC serves as a secondary doctrinal standard in Presbyterian churches that retain their biblical fidelity.

The WLC Q&As 65–81 relate to the application of redemptive benefits which Christ confers on believers in their union with him. Specifically, WLC 65 notes that believers (members of the invisible church) *enjoy* union and communion with Christ in grace and glory. WLC 69 asks and answers the following question:

> Q. 69. What is the communion in grace which the members of the invisible church have with Christ?

> A. The communion in grace which the members of the invisible church have with Christ, is their partaking of the virtue of his mediation, in their justification, adoption, sanctification, and whatever else, in this life, *manifests their union with him.*[29]

As with Calvin and Marshall, the Westminster divines in WLC 77 honor the Chalcedonian formula of "distinct, yet inseparable" benefits

---

28. We now have many resources that help us understand the historical and theological context in which the Westminster assembly met. See John V. Fesko's *The Theology of the Westminster Standards: Historical Context and Theological Insights* (Wheaton, IL: Crossway, 2014); Robert Letham's *The Westminster Assembly: Reading its Theology in Historical Context.* Westminster Assembly and the Reformed Faith series (Phillipsburg, NJ: P&R Publishers, 2009); and Chad Van Dixhoorn's *The Minutes and Papers of the Westminster Assembly, 1643–1653.* 5 vols. (Oxford, UK: Oxford University Press, 2012), and his *Confessing the Faith: A Reader's Guide to the Westminster Confession of Faith* (Carlisle, PA: Banner of Truth, 2014). These are especially attuned to the original historical context which sets linguistic and conceptual boundaries around the possible meaning of the text. Much of this work arises from the revolution in church history/historical theology studies under the pioneering work of Richard Muller. There are many more articles and books that deal with the theological content of the standards.

29. Emphasis mine.

within union with Christ:

> Q. 77. Wherein do justification and sanctification differ?

> A. Although sanctification *be inseparably joined with* justification, yet they differ, in that God in justification imputeth the righteousness of Christ; in sanctification his Spirit infuseth grace, and enableth to the exercise thereof; in the former, sin is pardoned; in the other, it is subdued: the one doth equally free all believers from the revenging wrath of God, and that perfectly in this life, that they never fall into condemnation; the other is neither equal in all, nor in this life perfect in any, but growing up to perfection.[30]

We see that while there has been variation among the theologians and the *Westminster Larger Catechism* at points, there is also a strong family resemblance. You cannot enjoy the benefits of redemption without being joined to Christ who procured those very benefits. You cannot enjoy the *benefits* without being united to the *Benefactor*. Rather than one benefit being so stressed that the others are forgotten, a proper emphasis on union with Christ while holding to the distinction between each of the blessings of redemption maintains a proper biblical balance. That balance, we shall see, is not always recognized or prized.

Contemporary Discussions of Union with Christ in Reformed Circles

There has been a virtual renaissance of scholarly investigation of the doctrine of union with Christ from the biblical, systematic, as well as historical sides of the question.[31] In the midst of this rediscovery of

---

30. Emphasis mine.
31. For instance, see J. Todd Billings, *Calvin and Participation: The Activity of Believers in Union with Christ*. Changing Paradigms in Historical and Systematic Theology series. (Oxford, UK: Oxford University Press, 2008) and *Union with Christ: Reframing Theology and Ministry for the Church* (Grand Rapids, MI: Baker, 2011); Constantine Campbell, *Paul and Union with Christ: An Exegetical and Theological Study* (Grand Rapids, MI: Zondervan, 2012); Robert Letham, *Union with Christ: In Scripture, History, and Theology* (Phillipsburg, NJ: P&R Publications, 2011); Marcus Peter Johnson, *One with Christ: An Evangelical Theology of Salvation* (Wheaton, IL: Crossway, 2013); Dennis E. Tamburello, *Union with Christ: John Calvin and the Mysticism of St. Bernard*. Columbia Studies in Reformed Theology series (Louisville, KY: Westminster John Knox Press, 1994); Grant Macaskell, *Union with Christ in the New Testament* (Oxford, UK: Oxford University Press, 2014); Mark A. Garcia, *Life in Christ and the Twofold Grace in Calvin's Theology*. Studies in Christian History and Thought series (Carlisle,

the centrality and significance of union with Christ for doctrine and life, disagreement about the relationship of union with Christ and the various discrete redemptive benefits has plagued Reformed theological discussion.[32] Older conversations about the doctrine of union include insights offered by neo-orthodox theologians such as Karl Barth and his Scottish disciple Thomas F. Torrance. Historical examinations of the doctrine of union in such thinkers as Calvin or Edwards have not escaped the well-known Calvin vs. the Calvinists dispute. Differences over the value of biblical theology (also known as redemptive-historical theology) in relation to systematic theology have also contributed to debate. One scholar even suggested that there was a "New Perspective on Calvin" analogous to the New Perspective(s) on Paul.[33] Other subsidiary controversies have fed the streams of discussion of the importance of union with Christ.

The most significant disagreement surrounds the relationship of union to justification. On the one side are those, such as the present author, who more or less follow Calvin's model of the centrality of union and the twofold blessing of God. On the other side are those who either

---

UK: Pasternoster, 2008); William B. Evans, *Imputation and Impartation: Union with Christ in American Reformed Theology*. Studies in Christian History and Thought series (Carlisle, UK: Paternoster, 2009); Michael S. Horton, *Covenant and Salvation: Union with Christ* (Louisville, KY: Westminster John Knox Press, 2007); Richard B. Gaffin, *Resurrection and Redemption* (Phillipsburg, NJ: P&R Publishing, 1987) and *By Faith, Not by Sight: Paul and the Order of Salvation*. 2nd ed. (Phillipsburg, NJ: P&R Publishing, 2013); K. Scott Oliphint, ed., *Justified in Christ: God's Plan for Us in Justification* (Fearn, Ross-Shire, UK: Christian Focus/Mentor, 2007); Lane G. Tipton and Jeffrey C. Waddington, eds. *Resurrection and Eschatology: Theology in Service to the Church: Essays in Honor of Richard B. Gaffin, Jr.* (Philippsburg, NJ: P&R Publishing, 2008); and Hans Burger, *Being in Christ: A Biblical and Systematic Examination in a Reformed Perspective* (Eugene, OR: Wipf & Stock, 2009). This selection is not exhaustive.

32. In addition to the titles mentioned above, see John V. Fesko, *Justification: Understanding the Classic Reformed Doctrine* (Phillipsburg, NJ: P&R Publishing, 2008); and R. Scott Clark, *Recovering the Reformed Confession: Our Theology, Piety, and Practice* (Phillipsburg, NJ: P&R Publishing, 2008), *Casper Olevian and the Substance of the Covenant: The Double Benefit of Christ*. Reformed Historical-Theological Studies series (Grand Rapids, MI: Reformation Heritage Books, 2008), and R. Scott Clark, ed., *Covenant, Justification, and Pastoral Ministry: Essays by the Faculty of Westminster Seminary California* (Phillipsburg, NJ: P&R Publishing, 2007). Again, there are many other titles that could be included *ad infinitum*.

33. See Thomas L. Wenger, "The New Perspective on Calvin: Responding to Recent Calvin Interpretations," *Journal of the Evangelical Theological Society* 50/2 (June 2007): 311–28.

want to protect or privilege justification within union or who deny definitive sanctification and subsume it under the aegis of justification. It is safe to conclude, I think, that all sides want to protect the gains of the Protestant Reformation and the rediscovery of the doctrine of justification. But the nexus of the dispute resides in whether or not a recognition of the centrality of union with Christ eclipses justification or not. *It need not and it ought not.* We can and ought to recognize that union with Christ is the umbrella context in which the various redemptive benefits come to the believer. While it is true that a concern with union with Christ has led some New Perspective(s) on Paul scholars and those whom they have influenced to blur the proper biblical distinction between justification and sanctification, this is not a necessary entailment of emphasizing the biblical focus on the fact that the redemptive benefits come to us as we are united to Jesus Christ.

If we take Calvin's view as instructive, we see that the twofold blessing addresses the problems brought about by sin. Justification corrects the guilt of sin. Sanctification corrects the corruption of sin. If we expand the blessings to address alienation, as the Westminster divines appear to do, then adoption answers that problem. To note that the benefits are distinct, yet inseparable does not undermine the integrity of either justification or sanctification. Only if one assumes that justification forms the foundation or basis of sanctification does a problem arise. And the twofold blessing is really talking about justification and *definitive* sanctification, *not* progressive sanctification.[34] There is a real sense in which justification provides the *existential foundation* for progressive sanctification. But justification and definitive sanctification are distinct, inseparable, and, I would add, simultaneous. The same would

---

34. I should add that recognizing the relatively recent vintage of the formal definition and destinction of definitive sanctification from positional and progressive sanctification does not invalidate its truthfulness or improvement over older formulations. If age was the only factor in assessing the validity of a doctrinal formulation that would be tantamount to chronological snobbery in reverse. Our culture typically commits this fallacy by assuming that what is newer is truer and what is latest is greatest. That form of chronological snobbery is no better. It is true that older formulations have the weight of longer periods of acceptance and usage within the church. This is no small thing or minor matter. But dislike for the theologian who first put a name to a doctrine or preference for an older formulation simply because it is older does not establish its biblical bona fides. Those who reject definitive sanctification have an obligation to demonstrate its lack of biblical foundation.

be true for adoption.

To affirm that union with Christ is the proper context in which the believer experiences justification is not to suggest, as Albert Schweitzer once did, that justification is a "subsidiary crater" for Paul or a temporary tactic at best formulated to deflect the legalistic Judaizers.[35] Additionally, talk of justification providing the forensic basis of union appears to be a move toward Lutheranism away from the genius of the Reformed (biblical) perspective. It is logically confusing. How can justification be grounded in the Christ of our union and also be its foundation? Admittedly we do need to recognize that the point of dispute in the Reformation was the doctrine of justification (among others). However, given the systematic and interrelated nature of all biblical doctrine, a misunderstanding of one doctrine leads to a misunderstanding of all doctrine. To recognize that union with Christ is the "central soteric blessing" entails that the twofold or threefold blessing is also central![36]

Practical Effects of Union with Christ

What does all this mean? Here are just a few observations:

1. Recognition of the centrality of union with Christ helps us to remember that we cannot enjoy the benefits of redemption without the Redeemer.

2. Recognition of the centrality of union with Christ *keep the discrete redemptive benefits together while allowing each its proper significance.*

3. Recognition of the centrality of union with Christ allows us more easily to see how redemption *addresses* and *surpasses* the fall into sin.

4. Recognition of the centrality of union with Christ enables us to *keep together* the promises of the gospel and the resulting commands and expectations that follow.

---

35. Albert Schweitzer, *The Mysticism of Paul the Apostle.* The Albert Schweitzer Library series (William Montgomery, tr. Jaroslav Pelikan, introduction. Baltimore, MD: The Johns Hopkins University Press, 1998), xvi.

36. But not in the sense understood by nineteenth century German historical theology where it was thought that various doctrinal systems were *deduced from* a "central dogma."

5. Recognition of the centrality of union with Christ keeps the focus on the *eschatological superabundance* of redemption. Redemption is not merely remedial.

Conclusion

Is union with Christ central? Yes. Does this recognition *eclipse* justification or any other redemptive benefit? Not when we understand each in its proper significance. When the believer is united to Christ by Holy Spirit-wrought faith, he is justified, adopted, and sanctified. To be justified is not to be adopted. To be adopted is not to be sanctified. To be sanctified is not to be justified. To seek to possess any of these blessings of salvation apart from their proper biblical context in union with Christ is, as John Calvin warned us many years ago, "to tear Christ into pieces."[37]

Related Episodes

- By Faith, Not by Sight with Richard B. Gaffin, Jr.
  » http://reformedforum.org/ctc319
- Issues in Systematic Theology
  » http://reformedforum.org/ctc191
- Theology and Ministry in Light of Union with Christ with Todd Billings
  » http://reformedforum.org/ctc221
- Union with Christ with Lane Tipton
  » http://reformedforum.org/ctc200
- Union with Christ, A Response with Michael Horton
  » http://reformedforum.org/ctc207
- Justification and Union with Christ with Tipton and Horton
  » http://reformedforum.org/ctc213
- Justification Sola Fide with Tipton
  » http://reformedforum.org/ctc257
- Union with Christ and Twofold Grace with Mark Garcia
  » http://reformedforum.org/ctc26
- The Justification Landscape with Mark Garcia
  » http://reformedforum.org/ctc162

---

37. Calvin, *Institutes*, III.xvi.1 (1:798).

- John Flavel and Union with Christ with William Edwards
  » http://reformedforum.org/ctc246
- Union with Christ and the Incarnation with Marcus Johnson
  » http://reformedforum.org/ctc345
- Union with Christ and the Body of Christ with Marcus Johnson
  » http://reformedforum.org/ctc346
- A Biblical Overview of Union with Christ, Richard B. Gaffin, Jr.
  » http://reformedforum.org/rfs10
- Union with Christ and Regeneration, Lane G. Tipton
  » http://reformedforum.org/rfs11
- Union with Christ: The Good Work Begun, Richard B. Gaffin, Jr.
  » http://reformedforum.org/rfs12
- Union with Christ and Sanctification, Lane G. Tipton
  » http://reformedforum.org/rfs13
- Questions and Answers on Union with Christ
  » http://reformedforum.org/rfs14
- Union with Christ: The Gateway into Fellowship with the Triune God
  » http://reformedforum.org/rfs15
- Union with Christ and the Gospel, Lane G. Tipton
  » http://reformedforum.org/rfs16
- Union with Christ and Glorification, James J. Cassidy
  » http://reformedforum.org/rfs17

6

WORSHIP, COVENANT, AND ESCHATOLOGY

GLEN J. CLARY

R EFORMED BIBLICAL THEOLOGY, in the tradition of Geerhardus Vos, emphasizes the centrality of two biblical motifs, namely, covenant and eschatology. When God created man, he entered into a covenant of life with him, which was the basis of the loving fellowship and communion with God that Adam enjoyed in the Garden (WSC 12; WLC 20; WCF 7:1). However, this original communion with God was not the highest form of communion possible. By his personal, exact, and entire obedience to God, Adam could have attained a higher state of perfection. He could have entered into a state of glory and enjoyed communion with God in its consummative form. The apostle Paul tells us that what the first Adam could have received, our Lord Jesus Christ, the second Adam, obtained in his resurrection from the dead (1 Cor 15:42–49). And all who are united to Christ through faith will fully share this blessing with Christ in the age to come, the eschaton (1 Cor 15:22, 50–55).

The covenant-communion bond that God established with Adam at the beginning had an eschatological orientation, but it also had a liturgical nature. "Man's chief end [was] to glorify God and to enjoy him forever" (WSC 1). This simple statement encapsulates the true essence and aim of worship, which is to glory and enjoy God. In the worship of God, man fulfills the purpose for which he was created; the Creator and the creature commune with one another in a manner that expresses the covenant-communion bond that unites them in loving fellowship. Communion with God in worship is of the very essence of the covenant and the goal of man's eschatology.[1] This communion with God, which was lost in the fall, has now been restored and perfected through the person and work of Jesus Christ, who "abolished death and brought life and immortality to light through the gospel" (2 Tim 1:10). In fulfilling the promises of the covenant of grace, Christ restored and perfected communion with God and, therefore, made it possible for us to worship the Father in an eschatological mode of worship, which Christ described as "worship in Spirit and truth" (John 4:23–24).

In this chapter, we will endeavor to demonstrate the covenantal and eschatological dimensions of worship by examining two key texts: the worship of Israel at Mt. Sinai (Exod 24:1–11), and the conversation about worship that Christ had with the Samaritan woman at the well (John 4:20–24). Reformed seminaries commonly treat the subject of worship as an applied science, a practical discipline, instead of a theological one. Worship as one of the theological *loci* has not found a permanent place in the seminary curriculum. Liturgical studies are designed to answer the question "*how* to worship" rather than "*what* is worship." The problem with teaching worship from this perspective is that it fails to "set forth the meaning of worship either as a whole or in its separate parts."[2] Our hope is that this brief study of the covenantal and eschatological dimensions of worship will encourage readers to pursue the study of worship as a theological discipline and especially to consider how the insights of Reformed biblical theology might be brought to bear on the subject of worship.

1. See Danny Olinger, ed., *A Geerhardus Vos Anthology* (Phillipsburg, NJ: P&R, 2005) 1–27.

2. Alexander Schmemann, *Introduction to Liturgical Theology* (Crestwood, NY: St Vladimir's Seminary Press, 2003) 9.

Worship and Covenant

Reformed theologians commonly define worship and the various elements of worship in covenantal terms. The Westminster divines, for example, defined the sacraments as "signs and seals of the covenant of grace" (WCF 27:1). The divines also characterized public worship as "communion with God in his public ordinances."[3] Such communion, they explained, was established on the basis of God's covenant bond with his people (cf. WCF 7:1; WLC 20). Hence, public worship may be defined as "covenantal communion between God and his people in his public ordinances."[4] That is, when the saints gather for worship, God meets with them and communes with them, and they with him in a manner that expresses and nurtures the covenant-communion bond that unites them in loving fellowship.

One redemptive-historical event that highlights the covenantal nature of worship is the assembly of Israel at Mt. Sinai. This prototypical assembly (*qahal* in Hebrew, *ecclesia* in Greek) serves as the model for the sacred assemblies of Israel throughout the Old Testament. The biblical-theological roots of the meaning of the word "church" (*qahal, ecclesia*) may be traced back to Sinai.[5] As Edmund Clowney observed, "the *ecclesia* of God is that assembly before the Lord of which Sinai was the great pattern."[6] The author of Hebrews compares and contrasts the Sinai assembly (the old covenant *qahal*) with the new covenant *ecclesia*, which he characterizes as a heavenly assembly gathered for worship on God's holy mountain (Heb 12:18–29).

The significance of the Sinai assembly for worship is underscored, first of all, in the giving of the Ten Commandments (Exod 20:1–17). The first commandment demands absolute and exclusive loyalty to Yahweh and prohibits the worship of any other god. The second prescribes the true worship of Yahweh and forbids the false worship of him. The

---

3. From "The Directory for the Publick Worship of God" in *Westminster Confession of Faith* (Glasgow: Free Presbyterian Publications, 1997), 386.

4. From the Orthodox Presbyterian Church's Directory for Worship; see *The Book of Church Order* (Willow Grove, PA: The Committee on Christian Education of the OPC, 2015) 125.

5. See Edmund Clowney, *The Church* (Downers Grove, IL: IVP, 1995), 30; and Clowney, "Toward a Biblical Doctrine of the Church," *WTJ* 31 no. 1 (1968): 22–81.

6. Clowney, "Toward a Biblical Doctrine," 34.

third requires the Israelites to call upon the name of Yahweh and forbids any profane use of his name.[7] The fourth enjoins the observance of the Sabbath as a holy day consecrated for the purposes of rest and worship. Thus, in the first four commandments, we discover two critical things: (1) worship is not left to the inventions of man but is regulated by God, and (2) only that worship which God himself has prescribed is acceptable to him.[8]

In addition to the Decalogue, the significance of the Sinai narrative for worship is highlighted in the covenant-making ceremony of Exod 24:1–11. The ratification of the Sinai covenant involved a complex ritual that was carried out in the context of worship. The sacrifices (v. 5), the reading of Scripture (v. 7), the sprinkling of blood (vv. 6, 8), and the sacred meal (v. 11) were constitutive parts of the ratification ritual, but they were also acts of worship.[9] Moses, Aaron, Nadab, Abihu, and seventy of the elders of Israel were summoned to ascend Mt. Sinai and worship the LORD. Moses alone was permitted to draw near to Yahweh; the priests and elders had to worship from a distance, at a lower point on the mountain.[10] The other Israelites had to stay clear of the mountain altogether (Exod 24:1–2).[11]

The twelve pillars erected at the foot of the mountain, symbolizing the twelve tribes of Israel, highlight the covenantal nature of the event (Exod 24:4). As Thomas Dozeman explains, the pillars "suggest some form of a covenant ceremony. A pillar provides the witness to a covenant between Jacob and Laban in Gen 31:45–54."[12] The identity of the "young men" sent to offer burnt offerings and sacrifice peace offerings is undisclosed (Exod 24:5). The term "young men" likely refers to a definite group of attendants who formed a makeshift priesthood until it was replaced by the Levitical priesthood, which had not yet been

---

7. Calling upon the name of the Lord is an act of worship; cf. Gen 4:26; 12:8; Ps 105:1.

8. Cf. WCF 21:1.

9. See Carol Meyers, *Exodus* (Cambridge: Cambridge University Press, 2005), 205.

10. See Thomas Dozeman, *Exodus* (Grand Rapids, MI: Eerdmans, 2009), 563; cf. Victor Hamilton, *Exodus* (Grand Rapids, MI: Baker, 2011), 438.

11. On the connection between these three groups of people at Sinai and the threefold structure of the tabernacle, see Angel Rodriguez, "Sanctuary Theology in the Book of Exodus," *Andrews University Seminary Studies* 24 (1986):127–45.

12. Dozeman, 565.

established.[13]

The purpose of the two kinds of sacrifices in the ratification cere-mony is not explicitly stated (Exod 24:5).[14] With a burnt offering, the victim was "wholly consumed on the altar."[15] With a peace offering (also rendered "well-being offering" or "fellowship offering"), a portion of the victim was later eaten by the worshiper. A peace offering represented a communal meal between the worshiper and God. The peace offerings at Sinai were most likely what the leaders of Israel ate on the mountain (Exod 24:11).[16] The sacrifices at Sinai were apparently offered for both expiation and consecration. Sprinkling the blood on the altar achieved the former; sprinkling of the blood on the people, the latter (Exod 24:6, 8).[17]

The focal point of the covenant ratification ceremony is recorded in vv. 7–8:

> [Moses] took the Book of the Covenant and read it in the hearing of the people. And they said, "All that the LORD has spoken we will do, and we will be obedient." And Moses took the blood and sprinkled it on the people and said, "Behold the blood of the covenant that the LORD has made with you in accordance with all these words" (Exod 24:7–8).

The Book of the Covenant apparently contained the words and ordi-nances of the LORD that Moses had written down (cf. vv. 3–4).[18] The

---

13. See Hamilton, 438–39; Dozeman, 561; John Mackay, *Exodus* (Scotland: Men-tor, 2001) 418.

14. See Hamilton, 441; J. Gerald Janzen, *Exodus* (Louisville, KY: Westminster John Knox Press, 1997) 186. The repetition of the same two offerings in the story of the golden calf in Exod 32:6 is significant; see Dozeman, 565.

15. Dozeman, 565.

16. See Dozeman, 565.

17. It is noteworthy that Heb 9:22 and Matt 26:28 ascribe "to the blood an expiatory function" (Hamilton, 442). Likewise, Targums Pseudo-Jonathan and Onkelos interpret the sprinkling of the altar in Exod 24:6 as expiatory. "Moses took half the blood and put it on the altar to make atonement for the people"; see Margaret Barker, *Temple Themes in Christian Worship*, (Edinburgh: T&T Clark, 2007), 173. Cf. Dozeman, 565–66; and Jacob Milgrom, *Leviticus 1–16* (New Haven, CT: Yale University Press, 1998), 528–29.

18. "The expression 'Book of the Covenant' occurs in only one other context in the Hebrew Bible: Josiah's finding it in the temple prompts his religious reform (2 Kgs 23:2, 21). The repetition creates a literary relationship between the Jerusalem temple, the Book of the Covenant, and the foundational ceremony of covenant in the wilderness at the divine mountain"; Dozeman, 566; cf. Hamilton, 441.

declaration of the covenant marks a decisive moment in the ratification ceremony. By reading the Book of the Covenant, Moses formally
identified the parties and proclaimed the promises, stipulations, and
sanctions of the covenant.[19] The Israelites responded by taking a vow
of obedience; "All that the LORD has spoken we will do, and we will be
obedient" (Exod 24:7). This echoes their earlier vow taken upon their
arrival at Sinai (Exod 19:8). "The repetition of the people of the same
response . . . marks the beginning and end of the one great covenant
event."[20]

The covenant, having been proclaimed by Moses and accepted by
the people, was formally ratified by the application of "the blood of
the covenant" to both parties (Exod 24:6, 8).[21] The blood ritual began
when Moses divided the blood in half (signifying the two parties) and
sprinkling one portion on the altar, symbolically standing in the place
of God, and the other portion on the people.[22] This dual application
of the blood of the covenant joined both parties together in a covenant
bond of communion and fellowship.[23] As noted above, one of the purposes of sprinkling the blood on the people was to consecrate them as
holy to the Lord. It was a purification ritual. The application of blood
to both altar and people has only one parallel in the Hebrew Bible,
namely, the ordination ceremony of the priests (see Exod 29:19–20;
Lev 8:22–30). Dozeman explains the significance of this point for the
covenant ceremony:

> The parallel to Lev 8:22–30 underscores the purifying role of the ritu-
> al, preparing the people to live in proximity to holiness. The purifica-
> tion of the people allows the drama of theophany to progress beyond
> Exod 19:16–19, when Yahweh ceased the divine descent because of
> the lack of safeguards to protect holiness (19:20–24). The purging of

---

19. See Brevard Childs, *The Book of Exodus* (Louisville, KY: Westminster John Knox
Press, 2004), 506.

20. Childs, 503.

21. "The blood of the covenant" only occurs in one other Old Testament text (Zech
9:11). "The prophet Zechariah develops the theme of purification and theophany into
an eschatological vision of salvation when the 'blood of the covenant' prompts God to
refashion the creation and, in the process, to rescue the Israelite people from slavery
(Zech 9:9–13)"; Dozeman, 566.

22. Cf. Childs, 506; Dozeman, 565–66; Mackay, 420.

23. Cf. Hamilton, 440–41; Janzen, 186; Martin Noth, *Exodus* (Philadelphia, PA:
The Westminster Press, 1962), 198.

the people with the "blood of the covenant" does not allow them to feast with God on the divine mountain (24:9–11), but it does prepare them to see the Glory of Yahweh on the mountain (24:12–18), and eventually in the altar before the tabernacle (Lev 9:23–24).[24]

The theological and liturgical significance of the blood ritual in Exod 24:6, 8 for Christian worship can be demonstrated by its connection to the eucharistic words of Jesus in the upper room. When Christ took the cup and said, "This is my blood of the covenant" (Matt 26:28; Mark 14:24), he echoed the words of Moses at Mt. Sinai, "This is the blood of the covenant" (Exod 24:8). Both Luke and Paul emphasize the eschatological character of the eucharistic saying by including the word "new"—"this cup is the *new* covenant in my blood."[25] Thus, one of the central elements of new covenant worship (namely, the Lord's Supper) derives its theological significance and liturgical formulation in part from the blood ritual in Exod 24.[26]

The worship service at Sinai reached a crescendo with a vision of God in his heavenly temple and a sacred meal eaten in the presence of God (Exod 24:9–11). As a sign and seal of the Sinai covenant, the communal meal on the holy mountain displayed and nurtured the covenant-communion bond and loving fellowship between God and his people.[27] The communal meal is the culmination of the ratification rites of the covenant ceremony.[28]

> Moses and Aaron, Nadab, and Abihu, and seventy of the elders of Israel ascended the mountain, and they saw the God of Israel. There was under his feet as it were a pavement of sapphire stone, like the very heaven for clearness.[29] But he did not send his hand against the

---

24. Dozeman, 566; cf. ibid., 562; Mackay, 420.

25. Luke 22:20; 1 Cor 11:25; cf. Jer. 31:30. See Dozeman, 567.

26. On the significance of Exod 24:8 for New Testament soteriology and worship, see Matt 26:28; Mark 14:24; Luke 22:20; 1 Cor 11:25; Heb 9:18–22; 10:29; 12:24; 13:20. Cf. Hamilton, 441; and Leon Morris, *The Apostolic Preaching of the Cross* (Grand Rapids: Eerdmans, 1956), 60–107.

27. On the use of meals in covenant ceremonies, see Hamilton, 443; Noth, 196; Childs, 507; Mackay, 422; and Dennis McCarthy, *Treaty and Covenant* (Rome: Pontifical Biblical Institute, 1981).

28. See Childs, 502.

29. The term translated "clearness" has two meanings: "clear" and "pure." "Both meanings may be functioning in Exod 24:10–11, where the imagery suggests that the vision of God on the heavenly throne is 'clear,' meaning unobstructed. It also indicates

leaders of the people of Israel. They beheld God, and ate and drank (Exod 24:9–11).

The worshipers on Mt. Sinai experienced a theophany of the highest order. It was as if the summit of the mountain had become heaven itself, and "here 'in heaven' the 'God of Israel' [was] present."[30] The leaders of Israel saw a vision of the heavenly temple, which served as the model for the earthly sanctuary, the construction of which is the main theme for the remainder of the book of Exodus.[31] The temple motif is indicated by the description of the sapphire stone under Yahweh's feet. As Dozeman explains,

> The "sapphire-like stone" under the feet of God is the precious stone, lapis lazuli, used in temple construction in the ancient Near East. The prophet Ezekiel envisions the throne of God with the same material (Ezek 1:26; 10:1). . . . [T]he blue color of lapis lazuli could also refer to the pinnacle of the temple. The blue of the temple pinnacle symbolized the connection between heaven and earth that allows for the descent of God into the earthly sanctuary. Thus the vision is of the divine temple. The additional description of the vision, "like the very heaven for purity," requires interpretation. . . . The translation "like the very heaven for purity" indicates that the veil between heaven and earth is momentarily lifted.[32]

The experience of the worshipers on the mountain is "so surprising and dangerous that it requires a footnote," namely, that God did not kill the leaders of Israel; "he did not send out his hand against" them (Exod 24:11).[33] Instead of death, which might be expected in such circumstances, the worshipers received a glorious vision of God and shared intimate fellowship with him in the form of a communal meal. This sacred feast on God's holy mountain was nothing less than a proleptic participation in the eschatological feast of salvation at the consummation of history.[34] In the book of Isaiah, we find a description of the feast that God will spread for all nations on Mt. Zion in the last days.

---

that the 'pure' environment of heaven has also momentarily engulfed the participants"; Dozeman, 567; cf. Janzen, 187.

30. Noth, 195.
31. See Dozeman, 567–68; Janzen, 185.
32. Dozeman, 567; cf. Meyers, 207.
33. See Dozeman, 568.
34. See Mackay, 422.

On this mountain the LORD of hosts will make for all peoples a feast
of rich food, a feast of well-aged wine, of rich food full of marrow,
of aged wine well refined. And he will swallow up on this mountain
the covering that is cast over all peoples, the veil that is spread over
all nations. He will swallow up death forever; and the Lord GOD will
wipe away tears from all faces, and the reproach of his people he will
take away from all the earth, for the LORD has spoken (Isa 25:6–8;
cf. Rev 21:1–4).

Both Moses and Isaiah describe sacred meals eaten in the presence of
the LORD on two different mountains, Sinai and Zion respectively. The
former was a proleptic participation in the latter; it was a true foretaste
of the age to come.[35] The worship of Israel at Mt. Sinai was a prophetic
sign of the Messianic age, which our Lord Jesus Christ inaugurated in
his first coming. Consequently, as Isaiah predicted, the nations are now
being invited, through the preaching of the gospel, to come to Mt.
Zion and feast on God's holy mountain.[36] At the second coming of
Christ, believers will share in this eschatological feast in its consummative form, but already, they enjoy a proleptic participation in it through
the sacrament of the Lord's Supper, which is a semi-eschatological feast.
The Lord's Table, to which all nations are invited through the gospel, is
a prophetic sign that the Lord who *will come* has *already come* to inaugurate his kingdom. It is a sign that the great feast at the end of the age
is already being served.

The tabernacle, constructed by the Israelites before leaving the
mountain, "was to be a perpetuation of the Sinai experience."[37] When
the Israelites departed, they took the heavenly temple with them in
the form of an earthly replica that served as a copy and shadow of the
original and through which they would participate in the worship of
the heavenly sanctuary. The same "glory of the LORD" that settled on
the mountain also filled the tabernacle and later the temple.[38] God's
presence in the sanctuary caused the Sinai theophany "to be repeated in
Israel's cultic life."[39] Hence, the covenant-communion service and even

---

35. See Mackay, 421; Janzen, 188.

36. Cf. Isa 2:1–4; 25:6–9; Matt 8:11; 28:19–20; Luke 14:12–24.

37. Rodriguez, 134.

38. Cf. Exod 24:16; 40:34–38; 1 Kgs 8:10–11; 2 Chr 5:14; 7:1–3; Isa 6:1; Ezek
43:4–5; 44:4.

39. R. E. Clements, *God and Temple* (Oxford, Basil Blackwell, 1965), 22.

the cultic theophany at Sinai were recapitulated in the ongoing worship
of Israel at the tabernacle/temple. The covenant-communion bond, established at Sinai, was renewed and nurtured in the liturgical life of
Israel. The worship of ancient Israel was an extension and perpetuation
of "the covenant experience of Sinai."[40] "Both Sinai and the sanctuary
were, in the first instance, places for communion of this covenant community with their divine Redeemer."[41]

One conclusion that we may draw from the worship of Israel at Sinai
is that public worship is, above all else, covenantal communion with
God in his public ordinances. The prototypical assembly at Sinai serves
as the model for tabernacle and temple worship throughout the Old
Testament and forms the theological and liturgical background of the
kind of worship that Christ established in the new covenant.

Worship and Eschatology

In his conversation with the Samaritan woman at the well, Jesus described the essential nature of new covenant worship as "worship in
Spirit and truth" (John 4:23–24). Jesus also differentiated this kind of
worship from that which was offered by both the Samaritans at Mt.
Gerizim and the Jews in Jerusalem (vv. 21, 23). Reformed theologians
have typically interpreted this differentiation as a contrast between external worship and internal worship, often expressing it in the form of
an anthropological dualism.[42] However, Jesus was not making an an-

---

40. Rodriguez, 135.

41. Rodriguez, 141.

42. See Craig Farmer, ed., *Reformation Commentary on Scripture: John 1–12* (Downers Grove, IL: IVP, 2014), 134–37. Vos rejected this interpretation; see Geerhardus Vos,
Biblical Theology (Carlisle, PA: The Banner of Truth Trust, 2000), 357; and Richard
Gaffin, ed., *Redemptive History and Biblical Interpretation: The Shorter Writings of Geerhardus Vos* (Phillipsburg, NJ: P&R, 1980), 346. "The older interpretation that worship
of the Father by ... 'spirit and truth' meant worshiping God with inwardness and sin-
cerity has now been almost completely abandoned in modern scholarly commentary";
Frederick Bruner, *The Gospel of John* (Grand Rapids, MI: Eerdmans, 2012), 269; cf.
ibid., 263. Likewise, Raymond Brown says, "Today most exegetes agree that in proclaiming worship in Spirit and truth, Jesus is not contrasting external worship with
internal worship. His statement has nothing to do with worshiping God in the inner
recesses of one's own spirit; for the Spirit is the Spirit of God, not the spirit of man, as
v. 24 makes clear. . . . An ideal of purely internal worship ill fits the NT scene with its
Eucharistic gatherings, hymn singing, baptism in water, etc. (unless one assumes that
John's theology is markedly different from that of the Church at large)"; Raymond

thropological distinction but a redemptive-historical one. The contrast he makes is between different modes of worship in two different eras of redemptive history. Jesus contrasts worship in the pre-eschatological age with worship in the eschatological age, which he came to inaugurate.[43]

Jesus informed the woman that "the hour is coming" when the dispute between the Jews and the Samaritans over the proper place of worship will be obsolete (John 4:21). In John's Gospel, "the hour" refers to the climactic moment when Jesus is glorified through his death, resurrection, and return to the Father, after which he sends the Holy Spirit.[44] "The hour" in view in John 4 is an eschatological marker that points to the decisive moment in redemptive history that inaugurates the last days. It marks the beginning of the end, the commencement in the history of salvation of the Messianic age.[45] It is noteworthy that Christ refers to "the hour" as both future and present; it "is coming and is now here" (John 4:23), indicating that the eschatological age is already a present reality because Christ is present.[46] The arrival of Christ signals the "inbreaking of the eschatological hour."[47] As Gail O'Day observed,

> "The hour is coming" is a word of promise and anticipation. The phrase "and is now here" signals that this anticipated time of promise and hope is upon us. . . . Jesus' words to the woman in vv. 21–24 focus on the power of eschatological newness—the inbreaking of the new age. . . . Jesus' presence in the world changes a word of anticipation—"the hour is coming"—to a word of fulfillment—"and is now here." The Samaritan woman's response in v. 25 indicates that she heard the eschatological promise of Jesus' words: "I know that Messiah is coming" (who is called Christ). "When he comes, he will proclaim all things to us." Jesus speaks of the coming hour; the wom-

---

Brown, *The Gospel According to John 1–12* (Garden City, NY: Doubleday, 1966), 180.

43. Cf. Vos, *Biblical Theology*, 357; Gaffin, *Redemptive History*, 346.

44. See John 5:25–29; 7:37–39; 16:2, 4, 21, 25, 32; 17:1. Cf. Marianne Thompson, *The God of the Gospel of John* (Grand Rapids, MI: Eerdmans, 2001), 214; Gerald Borchert, *John 1–11* (Nashville, TN: B&H, 1996), 207; Bruce Milne, *The Message of John* (Downers Grove, IL: IVP, 1993), 88.

45. It is noteworthy that the Samaritan woman knows Christ is "speaking about the eschatological age and that this age is the age of the Messiah"; see Gail O'Day, *Revelation in the Fourth Gospel* (Minneapolis, MN: Fortress Press, 1986), 72.

46. See O'Day, *Revelation*, 71; cf. Herman Ridderbos, *The Coming of the Kingdom* (Phillipsburg, NJ: P&R, 1962); Robert Kysar, *John* (Minneapolis, MN: Fortress Press, 1986), 66.

47. O'Day, *Revelation*, 52.

an speaks of the coming One. . . . The critical difference between
Jesus' words and the woman's words is that the woman does not seem
to grasp the eschatological immediacy so central to vv. 21–24. The
woman's words focus on "the hour is coming," but reflect nothing of
the "and is now here" of which Jesus speaks.[48]

Hence, the coming of Christ ushered in this new era of worship that
Christ described as "worship in Spirit and truth" in contrast to the worship of the previous age.[49] Those who worship the Father in "the hour"
that "is now here" must worship him "in Spirit and truth" (vv. 23–24).
This phrase must be interpreted within the context of the eschatological intrusion brought about by the glorification of Christ, especially
considering the fact that it is "the hour" of his glorification that makes
"worship in Spirit and truth" possible and necessary.

If worship "in Spirit and truth" describes the worship of the eschatological age inaugurated by Christ's coming, then what does "Spirit and
truth" mean?[50] Worship in this new age of redemptive history must be
characterized by "Spirit and truth" because it is an age of "Spirit and
truth." The phrase is descriptive of the Messianic age as a whole. With
that in mind, we should note that since this new era of redemptive
history cannot be separated from the person of Christ who inaugurated
it, the phrase "in Spirit and truth" should not be interpreted apart from
him.[51] This inseparable connection between the Johannine phrase and

---

48. O'Day, *Revelation*, 51–52; cf. Gail O'Day and Susan Hylen, *John* (Louisville,
KY, Westminster John Knox Press, 2006), 54; and Kysar, 66.

49. See Andreas Köstenberger, *John* (Grand Rapids, MI: Baker, 2004), 155; Herman
Ridderbos, *The Gospel of John* (Grand Rapids, MI: Eerdmans, 1997), 163; Borchert,
207; and Brown, 172.

50. The two nouns "Spirit" and "truth" are linked together by a single preposition
and form one complex idea. Even if they are not a hendiadys, as some have suggested,
they sustain an inseparable relationship to each other as two sides of the same coin. See
Kostenberger, 156–57; Ridderbos, *John*, 163; Brown, 180; D. A. Carson, *The Gospel
According to John* (Grand Rapids, MI: Eerdmans, 1991), 225; and Leon Morris, *The
Gospel According to John* (Grand Rapids, MI: Eerdmans, 1971), 271.

51. See Andrew Lincoln, *Gospel According to John* (London: Bloomsbury, 2005),
178; 182. "Jesus is the new focus of worship, just as earlier he was portrayed as the true
place of worship—the new tabernacle (1:14), the new Bethel or house of God (1:51),
and the new temple (2:19–22)"; ibid. 182. "Since Jesus is the giver of the Spirit and
the embodiment of the truth, worship in Spirit and in truth is also worship centred in
and mediated by Jesus"; ibid., 178. Rudolf Schnackenburg has even suggested that "in
Spirit and truth" is the Johannine equivalent of Paul's "in Christ." True worship "in the
Spirit is only possible in union with Christ. His glorified body is the holy temple of

the person of Christ points up a weakness in the common interpretation of John 4, which interprets it as a reference to internal or spiritual-
ized worship. As O'Day explains,

> Worship of the Father in spirit and truth does not point to an inter-
> nal, spiritualized worship that thereby makes the place of worship ir-
> relevant. Instead it points to a true and full worship of the Father that
> reflects a full knowledge of who the Father is and full communion
> with the Father. . . . The historical problem of Jewish verses Samaritan
> worship is transformed into a statement of the eschatological encoun-
> ter with divine reality. This eschatological mode of worship is possible
> now ("and now is") because Jesus and the gift of his revelation make
> the [S]pirit accessible. It is only through recognition of Jesus' identity
> and entry into relationship with him that one becomes a true wor-
> shiper. That God seeks those who worship in [S]pirit and truth (v.
> 23b) underscores that this worship is indeed present and accessible
> through one's present relationship with Jesus.[52]

O'Day is surely on the right track when she interprets "Spirit and truth"
in terms of the gift of the Holy Spirit and the revelation of God ("truth")
communicated through the person and work of Jesus Christ.[53] True
worship "is worship offered in and through Jesus Christ; only through
the truth he embodies, and the Spirit he imparts, can we know God
and worship him."[54] By sending the Holy Spirit and revealing the truth,
Christ is the one who establishes the true worship of the Father, and
only those who are "born of the Spirit" (John 3:5) and sanctified "in the
truth" (John 17:17) can "worship in Spirit and truth."[55]

The eschatological "hour" of Christ's glorification released "a new

---

God (2:21); true worship is performed in him. To this extent, the [in Spirit] of John is
akin to the [in Christ] of Paul. In any case true and acceptable adoration is only possible
through Jesus, the revealer and bringer of life (cf. 4:26; 6:63f.)"; Rudolf Schnackenburg,
Gospel According to John, vol. 1 (London: Burns and Oates, 1982), 439.

52. O'Day, *Revelation*, 70–71.

53. For an extensive argument in support of this interpretation, see Marianne
Thompson, 214–16. Kostenberger notes that the terms "spirit" and "truth" are "joined
later in the expression 'Spirit of truth,' referring to the Holy Spirit (see 14:17; 15:26;
16:13; cf. 1 John 4:6; 5:6; see also 2 Thess. 2:13). Though this may have been too advanced for the Samaritan woman, the present reference therefore seems to point John's
readers ultimately to worship in the Holy Spirit"; Kostenberger, 157.

54. Milne, 88.

55. See Schnackenburg, 437; Borchert, 208; Morris, 272; Thompson, 215; Rudolf Bultmann, *The Gospel of John* (Philadelphia, PA: The Westminster Press, 1971),
189–91.

work of the Spirit"; it supplied "the necessary medium and vehicle" through which worship in the Messianic age takes place.[56] The redemption accomplished by Christ and applied by the Spirit brings us into this eschatological realm in which we "worship the Father in Spirit and truth" (John 4:23).[57] In other words, during the semi-eschatological age between the first and second coming of Christ, worship takes place by the agency of and in the sphere of the Holy Spirit, who unites us to the person of Christ, the revealer and embodiment of the truth by which we are sanctified (John 17:17).[58]

In this regard, we should point up the Trinitarian significance of the saying of Jesus in John 4:23–24. Frederick Bruner has convincingly argued that "Father," "Spirit," and "Truth" in this text should be interpreted as a reference to the three persons of the Trinity. In John's Gospel, "we are obliged by John's consistent use of language to understand 'the Father' as God the Father, 'the Spirit' as the Holy Spirit, and 'the Truth' as Jesus the Son of God."[59] Andrew Lincoln explains the significance of this Trinitarian interpretation for new covenant worship; we "participate in worship," he writes, "that has clearly Trinitarian dimensions, because it is worship of the seeking Father, mediated by the person of Jesus, and enabled by the life-giving Spirit."[60] Many of the Church Fathers and Reformers affirmed this Trinitarian interpretation of John 4; unfortunately, however, modern biblical scholars tend to reject it as speculative and anachronistic, on the assumption that the doctrine of the Trinity is only a later church development.[61] Bruner is undoubtedly correct, however, in arguing that the apostle John, in ch. 4 of his Gospel, introduces to his readers "what the later Church will rightly cherish as the doctrine of 'the Trinity.'"[62] The nascent Trinitarian terminology of "Father," "Spirit," and "Truth" in John 4:23–24 is developed and

56. Thompson, 215
57. Thompson, 215.
58. See George MacGregor, *Gospel of John* (London: Hodder and Stoughton, 1927) 105. On the semi-eschatological nature of the present age, see Olinger, 18, 55, 91.
59. Bruner, 268–69.
60. Lincoln, 182. "True worship is accordingly the worship offered through the Son and in living faith-union with him by means of the Holy Spirit"; Milne, 88.
61. See Farmer, 134–37; Robert Letham, *The Holy Trinity* (Phillipsburg, NJ: P&R, 2004), 415–17.
62. Bruner, 263.

expounded more clearly as the Gospel of John unfolds (see especially chs. 14–16).

The transition from old covenant worship to new covenant worship was decisively marked by the eschatological hour of Christ's glorification and the ensuing bestowal of the Holy Spirit, who enables us to worship the Father in the realm of the Spirit and in full recognition of the person and work of Jesus Christ, the revealer and embodiment of divine truth, and the sum and substance of the shadowy ordinances that characterized worship under the law. The new state of affairs brought about by the revelation of Jesus Christ and bestowal of the Holy Spirit is nothing less than a definitive eschatological intrusion that rendered the earthly, typological, pre-eschatological worship of the old covenant totally obsolete. This accounts for the sharp distinction Christ made between worship in the old covenant and worship in the new, and why the Samaritan's woman question regarding the proper location of worship was obsolete. With the arrival of Christ, the types and shadows of the law give way to the reality to which they pointed. The temple of God in Jerusalem had reached its expiration date. The time had come for it to be replaced by the true, eschatological temple (cf. John 2:19–22).

The conclusion that we draw from John 4 is that new covenant worship is radically eschatological. To be sure, it has not yet reached its consummative state. That awaits the return of Christ. But with the definitive inbreaking of the age to come in the glorification of Christ, there is a radical and decisive break with the earthly, shadowy, temporary, pre-eschatological worship of the old covenant. The glory-cloud that rested on Mt. Sinai and filled the tabernacle/temple has now transformed the people of God themselves into a holy temple in which he permanently dwells (Eph 2:21–22). The covenantal communion enjoyed by the leaders of Israel on Mt. Sinai, as glorious as it was, pales in comparison to the unceasing, loving fellowship and covenantal communion that we now enjoy with our heavenly Father, through the merit and mediation of Jesus Christ, and by the agency of the Holy Spirit. In virtue of our union to the risen Christ, we already experience, in principle, the kind of communion with God that we will enjoy for all eternity in the age to come.

Related Episodes

- Pneumatology and Eschatology in the Light of 1 Corinthians 15:45 and 2 Corinthians 3:6–18
  » http://reformedforum.org/ctc367
- The Unfolding of Biblical Eschatology with Fowler White and Keith Mathison
  » http://reformedforum.org/ctc64
- 2016 Theology Conference—Image of God and Images of God: The Second Commandment and Reformed Worship
  » http://reformedforum.org/rf16_03_clary
- The Second Commandment and Images in Worship
  » http://reformedforum.org/ctc458
- The Regulative Principle of Worship with Darryl Hart
  » http://reformedforum.org/ctc236
- The Regulative Principle of Worship
  » http://reformedforum.org/ctc385
- Reformed Worship with Jon Payne
  » http://reformedforum.org/ctc68
- Calvin and the Sabbath with Richard B. Gaffin, Jr.
  » http://reformedforum.org/ctc455
- The Synod of Dort's Deliverance on the Sabbath with Danny Hyde
  » http://reformedforum.org/ctc450
- The Decalogue
  » http://reformedforum.org/ctc447
- The Prologue and First Commandment of the Decalogue
  » http://reformedforum.org/ctc454
- The Decalogue: The Second Word
  » http://reformedforum.org/ctc462
- The Decalogue: The Third and Fourth Words
  » http://reformedforum.org/ctc466
- The Mosaic Covenant as a Republication of the Adamic Covenant
  » http://reformedforum.org/ctc451
- The Law and Redemptive-History
  » http://reformedforum.org/ctc220

7

CITIZENS OF HEAVEN, STRANGERS ON EARTH

JAMES J. CASSIDY

WHAT IS THE nature of the church? How are we to answer the question? There are many different notions of what the church is. Some people think of a building. Others think of a group of people. Others still think of church leaders who wear garments and garbs. But what, biblically speaking, is the church at its very essence? In this chapter we will seek to get to the bottom of what exactly, according to Scripture and the Reformed tradition, the church is.

Our working thesis is that the church of Jesus Christ is a heavenly and eschatological reality. That is a fancy way of saying that we as the New Covenant church of God are those who live in the fulness of time (Gal 4:4; Eph 1:10). We are a people of the end times. Now, that phrase "the end times" in the American context often conjures up images of books and movies about the rapture which are more effective in frightening people than in edifying people. But that is not how we are using that phrase here. So, what do we mean when we say that the church of the Lord Jesus Christ is an "end times" people?

Let us frame the answer with a brief "redemptive-historical" sketch.[1]

---

1. When we say "redemptive-historical" here we simply mean how God works his

First, Jesus Christ came to inaugurate—or kick off—the end times as he came to fulfill all the promises of God given under the Old Covenant. He did this through his incarnation, life, death, and especially his resurrection.[2] That means that the end times are not, as such, a time in the future from our perspective. Rather, "these last days" have already arrived with the final spoken revelation of God in Jesus Christ (Heb 1:1–2). Second, those "last days," these "end times," continue and abide until "the last day" (John 6:39, 40, 44, 54; 11:24; 12:48). This is the consummation of what Jesus inaugurated at his first coming. And so we in Christ are his people upon whom the end of the ages has dawned (1 Cor 10:11).

And that means that there is an important difference between us as God's people now and God's people under the Old Covenant. Now this is not dispensationalism in disguise! No, in fact, God's people are one. There is only one covenant of grace and there is only one people of God extending from the Old Covenant into the New Covenant. There is only one way of salvation. Justification has always been by faith alone through grace alone, because of Christ alone! The people of God under the Old Covenant are no less the church than we are under the New.

Explaining the relation between the people of God in Old and New the Westminster Confession of Faith 7.6 is helpful: "There are not therefore two covenants of grace, differing in substance, but one and the same covenant, under various dispensations." But this fundamental continuity between the Old and New Covenants must never obscure the important discontinuity. And that discontinuity comes to the foreground when we speak about how to understand the church, particularly how we are to understand the church under the New and everlasting Covenant. At the heart of this discontinuity is eschatology.

---

redeeming grace in history. So, for example, we can say the Bible is a "redemptive-historical" book because it is essentially a history book which contains the story of how God unfolded his plan in time to redeem for himself a people through his Son Jesus Christ. So, when we speak about eschatology or the end times, we have in view the climax and culmination of that unfolding history. History, like all good stories, has a beginning and an end.

2. Very important here is the seminal work of Richard B. Gaffin, Jr., *Resurrection and Redemption: A Study in Paul's Soteriology*, 2nd ed. (Phillipsburg: P&R Publishing, 1987). Gaffin underscores and highlights the eschatological nature of the resurrection of Christ which inaugurates the end times.

Further explanation is in order.

From Gen 3:15 on, the Old Covenant people of God lived in and by the Covenant of Grace. But they lived in an administration of types and shadows. The substance is the same between Old and New. And that substance is Christ himself, revealed in the Covenant of Grace. The Old differs from the New not in substance but in how it was administered. So, WCF 7:6:

> This covenant was differently administered in the time of the law, and in the time of the Gospel: under the law it was administered by promises, prophecies, sacrifices, circumcision, the paschal lamb, and other types and ordinances delivered to the people of the Jews.

So, the people of God under the Old, were God's people "underage." (Gal 4:1–6) And with them the covenant was administered by promises and types. It was not administered as if it were the fulfillment of the Covenant. In other words, the means by which the Covenant of Grace was administered then were sub-, or pre-, eschatological. It was administered by earthly—as opposed to heavenly—pictures. They were the pictures, not the reality. They were promises, not fulfillments.

And so, in light of this the author to the Hebrews can speak about the Old as inferior to the new. In fact, the inferior is fading away and has become obsolete (Heb 8:13). Not that there is anything inherently deficient about the Old! But because of the arrival of the New the Old has been superseded. And this renders the old administratively obsolete. That is to say, the pictures have given way once and for all to the reality.

Some Exegetical Reflection on Philippians 3

Paul writes with this perspective in Philippians 3. Paul, in many of his letters but especially here is waging war against those of the "circumcision party." They are the ones who were saying that our salvation is dependent upon our keeping the Mosaic law, or the Old Covenant types and shadows. Of special focus in Paul's polemic is, of course, the practice of circumcision.

In 3:2 he warns the Philippians to watch out for the dogs. Who are the dogs? They are those who "mutilate the flesh." He is talking about the circumcision party, or the "Judaizers." And in v. 3 he speaks about the church in the New Covenant. The true church is not defined by circumcision or by any other aspect of the Old types, shadows, and pictures. Rather, the New Covenant people of God are those who are the real circumcision. Whether Jew or Gentile, the New Covenant people of God are characterized not by the law but by worship in the Spirit. That is to say, by worship that comes by the Holy Spirit. Or, to put it in the words of Jesus to the woman at the well, "But the hour is coming, and is now here, when the true worshipers will worship the Father in spirit and truth, for the Father is seeking such people to worship him." (John 4:23).

This is what Old Covenant worship and circumcision promised and foreshadowed. Old Covenant worship was typological. It was promising something better, namely the fulfillment of all God's promises in Christ! And now Christians, whether Jew or Gentile, worship no longer by the ceremonial laws but by and in the Holy Spirit of Jesus Christ. That worship then was shadowy—pre-eschatological. New Covenant worship now is worship in the splendor of the light of the substance of the Covenant of Grace, who is Jesus Christ!

In light of this, v. 3, Paul puts "no confidence in the flesh." This is the case despite the fact that if anyone has a reason for confidence in the flesh, he himself has more! He has, in his own body, all the marks of the Old Covenant types. He is circumcised, of the tribe of Benjamin, and a Pharisee! In fact, he knew exactly how to keep that law! He goes to far as to say he is blameless! (end v. 6). However, this righteousness—the kind that comes by the law—is regarded by Paul as rubbish!

Why? Is not the law good and holy? (Rom 7:12). Yes it is! But it was only a type and shadow of the substance. So Paul can say that he counts all those things as loss in "order that I may gain Christ and be found in him, not having a righteousness of my own that comes from the law, but that which comes through faith in Christ. . ." (Phil 3:8–9) He gives up the types, shadows, and pictures for the substance.

Imagine with me for a moment that you are separated from your spouse. He or she is far away. But your spouse mails you a picture of him- or herself, and that picture is a help to you. It is not the same as your spouse being there with you. But it is better than nothing, and it is all you have. You hang the picture up, and you look at it every time you miss them.

Then one day your spouse returns while you are there in your home staring at the picture. Your husband or wife walks through the door, but instead of getting up and dropping the picture and running and embracing the real person you ignore them, continuing to hold onto and staring at the picture.

That would be absurd! You would be so glad to see the real thing you would not care about the picture! You might regard that picture as worthy of the garbage in comparison to the reality! Now, certainly, you would never actually throw that picture out, because it is a picture of your beloved. But relative to having the real deal the picture no longer comforts and satisfies.

Paul, likewise, would never throw out the Old Covenant laws. But in comparison with the glory of Jesus Christ the Old pictures so pale in comparison it is almost like the pictures are worthy of only the garbage can. Everything in the Old Covenant was leading up to Christ. Therefore, Christ is the goal of the law. He is the final revelation of God. In past ages, God spoke in many places and in many ways through types and shadows. But in these last days he has spoken by his Son. Jesus is the eschatological revelation of God.

Now, it is in this context that Paul gives the exhortation he does in 17–21. So, what I would like to do now is unpack Paul's meaning in v. 20. And note that the "but" contrasts the believer from the enemies of the cross referred to in v. 18. These enemies set their minds on earthly things. It is said their god is their belly and their glory is their shame.

There is a great deal of debate on the meaning of v. 18. Many take it as a reference to people who live licentiously. They argue that the "belly-god" is a reference to gluttony, and the enemy's glorying in their shame is a reference to uncontrolled pleasure in sin. While it is true that such licentiousness is at enmity with Christ, most certainly Paul has in view the Judaizers he condemns as dogs in v. 2. If that is the case, then the belly-god is a reference to the scrupulous dietary laws kept by the Judaizers which caused a division between Jewish and Gentile believers. And the reference to "shame" is a word used to describe those parts of our bodies that are clothed (1 Cor 12:23). And if the shame is a reference particularly to the "unpresentable parts" of the man, then the glorying in it referred to is a reference to the Judaizer's trusting in circumcision for salvation. So, it is these Judaizers that are earthly-minded. They have their minds set still on the pictures. They are set still on the earthly types and shadows of the Old Covenant ceremonial laws.

But it is not merely the ceremonial laws. Because with the ceremonial also comes the civil aspects of the law which rendered the Jews a body-politic. In other words, the ceremonial laws and the continual observance of them in the New Covenant led the Christian-Jews in the church to a kind of idolatrous nationalism. To be circumcised was to be Jewish. And to be of the nation of Israel was to be in covenant with God.

But the nation of Israel as a body-politic was also a type and shadow. So the WCF 19.4 says, "To them also, as a body politic, He gave sundry judicial laws, which expired together with the State of that people; not obliging under any now, further than the general equity thereof may require." In other words, the Judiazers identified their citizenship with the earthly, shadowy, typological nation of Israel as a body-politic.

Going back to v. 20, contrary to that mindset which identifies with an earthly citizenship, Paul and the believers in Philippi identify their citizenship as being in heaven. The church of the Lord Jesus Christ, consisting of Jews and Gentiles and a people of every tongue and nation is a city-state which is other-worldly. Jesus' Kingdom is not of this world. This is what the epistle to the Hebrews means when it says, "For you have not come to what may be touched . . . But you have come to Mount Zion and to the city of the living God, the heavenly Jerusalem . . . Therefore let us be grateful for receiving a kingdom that cannot be shaken . . ." (12:18–28). Moses came to Mount Sinai. Israel came to and worshipped on an earthly mountain. But not us in the new covenant! No! We come to a heavenly city! A heavenly Jerusalem! An unshakable Kingdom! In other words, our citizenship is in heaven!

The new covenant is a covenant God has made with his church. It is a covenant which he has made with his heavenly Jerusalem. It is made with all those who are in Jesus Christ and who have come to the heavenly Jerusalem by faith. Therefore, this covenant is not made with any nation-state today. God's covenant of grace is not with the nation of Israel nor with any city, nation, or institution on earth. It is only with the Church of the Lord Jesus Christ.

The church is the City of God and she has been made such by grace. Believers are not citizens by right, but by God's absolute sovereign grace. What a relief this is! For this means that our weapons in this world are not of this world! This means our hope is not found in this world. The Kingdom of God does not advance with or by the ways and methods of this world. It does not advance by way of the sword or by military might. This Kingdom does not advance by means of lobbying in Washington, DC. It does not advance with political influence. It does not advance by means of the voting booth!

Now that does not mean don't go vote! Indeed, go vote! And lobby in Washington if you like too. Support the candidate of your choice! But just remember, America (or whatever nation you live in) is not your home. Heaven is your home. Heaven is your city. And heaven is where you have your citizenship. Here, however, we have no lasting city. Here, we have shakable kingdoms. But the Jerusalem that is above is unshakable and the results of any election can not and will not budge it an inch. Seismic shifts occur in the political realm regularly throughout the world. But not even the most earth shattering coup or revolution can shake the Kingdom of God.

Strangers on Earth

To have her citizenship in heaven means that the church is a stranger on the earth. She is a "resident alien." She sojourns on the earth as a pilgrim knowing that this is not her home. Once again, the author to the Hebrews is helpful:

> By faith he went to live in the land of promise, as in a foreign land, living in tents with Isaac and Ja-cob, heirs with him of the same promise. For he was looking forward to the city that has foundations, whose designer and builder is God. . . . These all died in faith, not having received the things promised, but having seen them and greeted them from afar, and having acknowledged that they were strangers and exiles on the earth. For people who speak thus make it clear that they are seeking a homeland. If they had been thinking of that land from which they had gone out, they would have had opportunity to return. But as it is, they desire a better country, that is, a heavenly one. Therefore God is not ashamed to be called their God, for he has prepared for them a city (Heb 11:9–12, 13–16).

This means that even Abraham was not looking for an earthly city. Many Christians today believe that God's promise to Abraham of a place is still unfulfilled. Consequently, they await the day when Jesus will return to set up his millennial kingdom on earth as he comes to Jerusalem to re-establish the Temple. They believe that a part of God's end time plan is to restore Israel to its rightful place as a dominant nation on the earth. Abraham, however, was not seeking an earthly country but a heavenly one.

Other Christians, besides the ones just mentioned, are also seeking an earthly country. They have a lot in common with the previous group in this regard (though they differ significantly on other matters!). While this group is not seeking Israel as a nation, they are seeking the establishment of God's Kingdom through the governments, rulers, and institutions of this world. They believe that God's people are meant to dominate the world, unbelief is to be radically suppressed, and righteousness will reign and usher in a great and prosperous time for the church. Here also their identifying the Kingdom of God with world's institutions is to forget the eschatological nature of the church under the New Covenant. For the city, the homeland, that we inherit is imperishable and incorruptible (1 Pet 1:4). We have now by faith, and we will have later by sight, that city which Abraham sought.

Application and Conclusion

Therefore, the church under the New Covenant is the people of God with a spiritual and heavenly nature. And that means that the activity of the church will be in consonance with its nature. If its nature is that of a heavenly, eschatological entity, then its ways and its methods will also be very different from that of this present age. The WCF, picking up on this idea of the distinctive nature of the New Covenant church's ways and methods, says,

> Under the Gospel, when Christ, the substance, was exhibited, the ordinances in which this covenant is dispensed are the preaching of the Word, and the administration of the sacraments of Baptism and the Lord's Supper: which, though fewer in number, and administered with more simplicity, and less outward glory, yet, in them, it is held forth in more fullness, evidence, and spiritual efficacy, to all nations. (WCF 7.6)

This is the mission of the church. This is how the church wages warfare today. She is to preach the Gospel to all the nations. She is to administer and receive the sacraments with preparation and by faith. She is to be earnest in prayer before the throne of grace.

This is not the wisdom of man or the ways of the world. The wisdom of man struggles to figure out how to outwit and outmaneuver his opponents in the political realm. The wisdom of man tries to figure out a way to save society. It takes up carnal weapons thinking it is fighting the cause of Christ. Because it looks weak the wisdom from God is foolishness to man. But what the world sees as weakness, the means of grace, is actually the power of God onto salvation.

Paul says, "For we do not wrestle against flesh and blood, but against the rulers, against the authorities, against the cosmic powers over this present darkness, against the spiritual forces of evil in the heavenly places" (Eph 6:12). Our enemies, most ultimately, are not governments or political parties (though they may certainly oppose us!). Our enemies are not the atheistic and secularist think tanks. They are not the liberal media or the many "-isms" of the world (though those -isms and their advocates oppose the truth of God's Word). Rather, our struggle and fight is against powers of darkness which are "in heavenly places." In other words, just as our citizenship is not of this world, so likewise our enemies are not of this world. Everyone and everything in this world which oppose Christ are the deceived followers of the Beast. Unbelievers, no matter how antagonistic to the Gospel, are to be loved, forgiven, and prayed for by us. (Matt 5:44; Luke 23:34). They should be the objects of our evangelistic efforts, not the targets of our derision.

So, since our enemies are in the heavenly places, and our citizenship is in heaven, that means the weapons we use to combat them must be heavenly and spiritual. Paul says, "For though we walk in the flesh, we are not waging war according to the flesh. For the weapons of our warfare are not of the flesh but have divine power to destroy strongholds" (2 Cor 10:5). In this way we bring every thought captive to obey Christ. We wage war with the weapons of the Word, Sacraments, and Prayer. In context Paul in 2 Cor 10 is referring to church discipline. And the judgment of God comes against the unrepentant sinner not by stoning, hanging, or burning. Rather it comes through the church's exercise of the keys of the Kingdom to bind or loose on earth what is bound or loosed in heaven.

But how does the church do that? It does it through its ordained officers, specifically elders, who bind and loose by way of verbal declaration. Presbyterianism is very clear that all church power is ministerial and declarative only. That is to say the elders of the church exercise their power not with earthly might and with legislative powers, but rather they serve the Word of God (ministerial) through declaring what God has said (declarative). And when the elders of the church declare an unrepentant person outside of the covenant community in a way that is in accordance with the Word of God, what they declare is true in both heaven and earth.

Lastly, the church being a heavenly and spiritual institution does not mean its weapons are invisible. No, in fact, quite the opposite. The church is a very visible entity. The church is not a collection of disembodied souls. The church is a redeemed people consisting of both body and soul. The church then is something we can see, experience, and have fellowship in. But further, faith comes by hearing which requires real flesh and blood ears and minds. And hearing comes by the Word of God preached which requires real flesh and blood preachers. And the sacraments are administered with real water, bread, and wine. You can taste, see, smell, and touch the means of grace! But what makes them heavenly and spiritual is not the elements themselves, but the Spirit of the resurrected and ascended Christ who works in and through them. That makes the means of grace distinctly eschatological weapons against evil forces in the heavenly places. They are tethered to the promises of God and the presence of the Spirit in and among the people of God. And their form also communicates this. Notice, they are bloodless rites. They lack, to use the words of the Confession, "outward glory." They are not impressive by earthly standards. And that is because, of course, their efficacy does not adhere to the world's ways and methods of efficiency. Rather, their efficiency is found in heaven, where we are seated with Christ. And that is who we are as the church. In Christ, we are citizens of heaven and strangers on the earth.

Related Episodes

- Dualities in Epistemology, Eschatology, and Citizenship
  » http://reformedforum.org/ctc243
- Pilgrims in a Foreign Land
  » http://reformedforum.org/ctc448

- Eschatology and the Christian Life
  » http://reformedforum.org/ctc252
- Charles Hodge and the Spirituality of the Church with Alan Strange
  » http://reformedforum.org/ctc443
- Francis Schaeffer's Christian Spirituality with William Edgar
  » http://reformedforum.org/ctc273
- Christ and Culture: Marriage as a Test-Case with Marcus Mininger
  » http://reformedforum.org/ctc465

8

Reformed Covenantal Apologetics

Jeffrey C. Waddington

I T WOULD SEEM to be a deliverance of *sanctified* common sense that
we Christians seek to defend the faith and evaluate and interact
with other philosophies and religions from the perspective of God's
Word as explicated in the Reformed confessions and catechisms. That
is, our apologetics *ought to be consistent with* our theology. Our theology
is ultimately derived from Scripture as read within the parameters of the
Reformed faith and is informed by the various theological disciplines
like church history, biblical exegesis and redemptive-historical theology,
systematics, and pastoral theology. In this chapter, I hope to make the
case for a Reformed covenantal apologetic[1] that flows from or accompa-
nies a Reformed confessional commitment.

I should note here at the outset that I am not merely arguing for a

---

1. Reformed convenantal apologetics is the recent designation for presuppositional
apologetics that owes its existence to the insight of Cornelius Van Til (1895–1987),
former professor of apologetics at Westminster Theological Seminary in Philadelphia
building on the work of theologians from Old Princeton and Old Amsterdam. I owe
the use of "covenantal apologetics" to K. Scott Oliphint. He has used the expression in
multiple places, but the fullest treatment is *Covenantal Apologetics: Principles and Practice in Defense of Our Faith* (Wheaton, IL: Crossway, 2013).

consistent Reformed way to defend the faith and critique various forms of unbelief. If the Reformed expression of the Christian faith were not *the* biblical form of Christianity, then this chapter would be a species of postmodern *perspectivalist* thinking.[2] That is, I would simply be *delimiting and defining* what Reformed Christianity is and how one can defend it against all other forms of unbelief and other forms of Christian belief. I want to make the stronger argument that Reformed Christianity *just is* biblical Christianity (all other forms *falling short* or suffering from *compromise*) and so the covenantal apologetic method is the *only fully legitimate way* to defend the faith and critique other beliefs. You might read this as a very arrogant comment for me to make. It is not intended to be that. What we know as the Reformed faith has been *revealed* to us by *grace*. We have *not* sat around and dreamed up this faith for ourselves. Had we done this we would have undoubtedly come up with a Christian faith more conducive to our sinful desires.

My goal in this chapter is to outline what covenantal apologetics looks like in terms of its shape and color, and where it depends on its Reformed theological foundation I hope to call attention to that fact. Covenantal apologetics is, it should be said, biblical, Trinitarian, Reformed, covenantal, redemptive-historical, and eschatological. I will explain each of these in turn in due course. So our way forward will be (1) to provide a basic outline of Reformed theology as it bears on apologetics, and (2) to offer a brief and simplified description of the three elements of a covenantal apologetic.[3] In the end I hope that you the reader will agree with me that the covenantal apologetic is *not just the best*, but the *only way* to carry out the apologetic task set for us in

---

2. Assuming these two words—postmodern and thinking—are not inherently antithetical and therefore self-contradictory. For earlier attempts to argue that the Reformed faith *just is* biblical Christianity, see B. B. Warfield, *Calvin as Theologian and Calvinism Today* (Philadelphia, PA: Presbyterian Board of Publication,1909), 23–24, *The Plan of Salvation* (Philadelphia, PA: Presbyterian Board of Publication, 2015); and the *Selected Shorter Writings of B. B. Warfield* (John E. Metter, ed., Phillipsburg, NJ: P&R Publishing, 2001), 1:389; J. Gresham Machen, *J. Gresham Machen: Selected Shorter Writings* (D. G. Hart, ed., Phillipsburg, NJ: P&R Publishing, 2004); and Cornelius Van Til, *The Defense of the Faith*. 4th ed. (K. Scott Oliphint. Ed., Phillipsburg, NJ: P&R Publishing, 1955, 2008), 306–44.

3. Please note this statement. Not everything that can be said about Reformed covenantal apologetics will be said.

Scripture.[4]

A Basic Outline of Reformed Theology for the Apologetic Task

Reformed theology is *deeply rich* and the study of it is *richly rewarding*. I trust this brief manifesto you hold in your hands from *Reformed Forum* (whether in print or electronic form) will give you a taste of the Reformed faith's depth and richness. Here I will follow the example of the late Cornelius Van Til, erstwhile professor of apologetics at Westminster Theological Seminary in Glenside, Pennsylvania just outside of Philadelphia. Dr. Van Til in his *The Defense of the Faith* lines out the pertinent theological foundation for a biblical apologetic. I would encourage you to read that chapter in his book as it more fully develops what I am saying here.[5]

We start with the doctrine of God. This is often called "theology proper" in systematic theology (or dogmatics) textbooks. The God of Scripture is Trinitarian. He is Father, Son, and Holy Spirit. One personal essence and three persons. God has been Triune from eternity. He has not evolved from an "undifferentiated monad" to one God in three persons.[6] He has always been one and three. He will always be three and one. It is true that God's revelation of this divine mystery was revealed over time. But we must not confuse the progressive nature of biblical revelation with some sort of notion where God evolves over time so that in his being there is a being "pole" and a becoming "pole."[7] That error goes by the names of process theism and open theism. It bears no rela-

---

4. I should also not be read as affirming that Christians in other apologetic schools never succeed in defending the faith or that they never attain to any sort of truth. That is not the case at all. God blesses the efforts of sincere Christians as they seek to defend the faith. And we can and ought to learn from others. As Dr. Van Til noted years ago, all sincere true Christians are Calvinists or Reformed at prayer (J. I. Packer echoed this thought many years later). We are talking systems of doctrine and methods for defending the faith now. Calvinsts or Reformed Christians are personally not as good as their theology or apologetic method. Non-Reformed Christians are often better than their theology.

5. Van Til, *Defense of the Faith*, 27–44.

6. I heard this expression in a sermon by J. Ligon Duncan, chancellor of the Reformed Theological Seminary organization, when he was pastor of First Presbyterian Church in Jackson, Mississippi some time ago.

7. "Pole" is the technical process philosophical and theistic language for ends of a spectrum in God's own being.

tion to the God of the Bible. The Trinitarian nature of God bears on the apologetic task quite directly. If the God of the Bible is the specific Trinitarian God (*this* God and not *that* one) then we as Christian apologists ought to seek to defend *this* God and *not* some *general abstract divine concept* that bears no *real extra-conceptual* relation to the real God who *is*. To put it another way: there is no "god" in reality that matches the concept of "god" in the mind of a generic theist. I would imagine that there are as many generic theists in hell as there are *a*theists—probably more so.[8] This also means that the way we practice apologetics should not follow what is usually referred to as the *classical* model.[9]

While this way of doing apologetics has an ancient pedigree it really is nothing more than an old error. Without going into great detail, classical apologetics seeks to defend the Christian faith in at least two steps: first it argues on the basis of shared philosophical principles for generic theism. On the same or related principles it will argue for the nature of creation and man in particular, and for the idea that this generic deity has communicated with "his" human creation. Next, this method examines the Bible to ascertain if it is just such a communication. At this point it resembles evidentialism in that it seeks to determine the Bible's historical veracity by means of working backwards from miracles and fulfilled prophecy through Jesus to Jesus' approbation of the Old Testament and his pioneering the way for the writing of the New Testament. In both of these apologetic approaches the apologist is assuming a neutral stance toward the God of the Bible and the Christian faith.

---

8. This is because if we fail to embrace Jesus Christ, the Son of God become man, then we are left in our natural state (in Adam) and therefore fall short of the glory of the Triune God. In other words, we have not believed the gospel around which the Scriptures cohere. Besides, the term "generic theist," as a matter of fact, covers all those who recognize the existence of some sort of being affirmed as a deity whether that "deity" conforms to the biblical norm and standard or not. I would go even further and note that none of us are really generic theists by birth. So, on the one hand, we may confess to being a generic theist, and on the other hand, the true knowledge of the Triune God that is implanted in us means we are not generic theists at all. We can only be generic theists by suppression of the truth as Paul notes in Rom 1:18–32.

9. There are many books, past and present, that helpfully classify the various apologetic schools of thought. Steven Cowan's *Five Views on Apologetics* (Grand Rapids, MI: Zondervan, 2000) is one of the best. Cowan has gathered together representatives of the five major traditions: presuppositional, classical, evidential, cumulative case, and Reformed Epistemological/Warrantism.

He or she is arguing *from* unbelief *to* the Christian faith.[10] The Bible, on the other hand, argues *from* God and the truth of biblical revelation.

We should also note that our understanding of who God is needs to take into consideration who God is in himself (in Latin, *in se*) and who he is *towards us* or *in relation to* his creation (in Latin, *quoad nos*). God is a necessary being who is fully complete and lacking nothing in himself. Historically theologians refer to this characteristic of God as his *aseity* (from the Latin for "of himself" or *a se*).[11] God does not need anything from us to make himself complete or complete*r*. God is *un*caused. He does *not* cause himself. All of creation, including us human beings, is *contingent*. That is, we are *not* necessary and we *depend upon* God and our created environment to live and flourish. In other words, we are *derivative*. We label this two level reality the *Creator/creature distinction*. This distinction will have ramifications for our knowledge of God and his revelation.

God created us in a relationship to him from the start. This relationship is often described as *covenantal*. A covenant is a binding agreement between two or more parties. Marriage is a covenant agreement. Unlike business contracts which involve two *equal* parties (all other things being equal), the covenant between God and Adam was not bilateral in establishment. God sovereignly instituted it with his creature Adam. Adam had to respond but he was not given an option to opt out should he want to. As I have already indicated above, we are dependent upon God for our existence or being. We are dependent upon God for our coming into being and for our continuance in existence. We are also dependent upon God for our knowledge of him and the world which he created and in which he placed us. We are surrounded by God and his communication with us. He communicated with Adam in the Gar-

---

10. For the Christian to argue *from* a so-called neutral stance is in fact to deny the existence of the Triune God and his Scriptural revelation. A neutral stance essentially involves denying the existence of God and the veracity and authority of his Word. I am speaking about the internal attitude of the Christian who seeks to make common ground with an unbeliever.

11. Richard Muller, *Dictionary of Latin and Greek Theological Terms: Drawn Principally Protestant Scholastic Theology* (Grand Rapids, MI: Baker Book House, 1996) provides an excellent resource for defining technical terms that date from the time of the Reformation and before that are useful to know for not only historical theology but also for contemporary Reformed orthodox constructive systematic theology.

den of Eden through creation (Rom 1:19–21) and that includes our *human* nature, specifically our minds and consciences. In other words, our very make-up or constitution reveals God to us. The apostle Paul tells us that God has also revealed how he expects us to live and behave before him and our fellow human beings. Theologians tell us that God has communicated with us through nature and through his Scripture. These are typically referred to as natural or general revelation on the one hand, and special revelation on the other. These are not competing kinds of messages from God but two media that were intended to function together as mutually reinforcing types of revelation. God spoke to Adam before the fall through his surroundings but he also addressed him verbally when he prohibited him from eating from the tree of the knowledge of good and evil (Gen 2:15–17).

Adam was created as a representative of the whole human race. He was a real historical individual man, but in the initial creation context he was created to represent the whole human race, all men, women, boys, and girls. Adam was also the father of the whole human race, joining with Eve the mother of all who live. But Eve was not a covenantal representative or what we like to call a *federal head.* There have only been two federal heads in the whole history of the human race: Adam and Jesus Christ.[12] God created Adam for fellowship. It is not as if God somehow was trying to fill a void in his own life. God had and has no such void to fill. God is Triune: Father, Son, and Holy Spirit and he exists in eternal felicity. Rather, God desires to communicate his holiness and righteousness and love (among other things) in a mutual bond of fellowship. Adam was created upright, with knowledge, righteousness, and holiness (Col 3:10 and Eph 4:24). But he was initially on probation. Adam owed perfect, perpetual, and personal obedience. He owed this to God as his Creator. We should also note that God had no obligation to enter into any kind of relationship with Adam (and Eve). He entered into this covenant relationship out of his mere good will, benevolence, and good pleasure.

Note that Adam was created utterly dependent upon his maker for everything: life, love, happiness, and knowledge. This is our relationship to God as he created Adam. In a further step of good will, God brought

---

12. See my chapter on union with Christ elsewhere in this book.

Adam's probation to a fine point of testing. He commanded Adam to refrain from eating from the tree of the knowledge of good and evil. How is that an act of kindness? God could have required the probation to go on forever, world without end. But he offered Adam confirmed blessing in a close bond of mutual fellowship without diminution.[13] As opposed to letting things go on indefinitely in a state of probation, God offered to Adam this opportunity to demonstrate his loyalty to God without any reservation whatsoever. This promised blessing (proffered opportunity for unmitigated blessing) is implied in the pronouncement of destruction for eating the forbidden fruit.[14] As we now know, Adam (and Eve) failed to sustain the test in the garden. Ever since then the human race has lived "east of Eden" under God's just sentence of wrath and judgment. This fall from God's creational favor resulted in guilt for disobedience to God's express command and his law written on the heart. It also resulted in the loss of the original holiness, righteousness, and knowledge and therefore in corruption of our whole human nature (including our *reasoning* capacity). Finally, because of the fall we are now alienated from God and are at rebellious enmity with him. This includes *deliberately suppressing* the knowledge of God that we have in *engraved* in our very nature (Rom 1:18ff). In order to recover what has been lost and to enter into the proffered opportunity for unmitigated divine blessing, we must now enter by means of another covenant representative or federal head, Jesus Christ. Thinking about it this way, union with Jesus Christ brings us to the unique bond of close communion with the Triune God which was originally offered to Adam. This blessed

---

13. Lane G. Tipton of Westminster Theological Seminary notes that this is a very personal form of God's *sacramental presence*. From unpublished lectures in his Van Til's Trinitarian theology PhD seminar in the fall of 2016.

14. If you have doubts about a permanent blessing being offered, as over against an ongoing probation, think about this: If the consequence for a temporal act of disobedience was eternal death, then the implication would seem to be an implicit promise of eternal life for a temporal act of obedience. It is recognized that Adam had no right to demand this plan from God. Adam could not demand "justice" in the face of God. God's reward is out of all proportion to Adam's act of obedience. But once God bound himself to Adam in this arrangement, God was committed to reward Adam. But as it turned out, Adam was disobedient. Consider also the role of the tree of life in the Garden of Eden and throughout the rest of Scripture (in the Psalms, Jeremiah, and Revelation). After the fall, God places cherubim and a flaming sword to block the way to the tree of life. In Rev 21–22 only those who have overcome (i.e., persevered) are given a right to access the tree of life in the New Jerusalem.

communion was proffered to Adam contingent upon his obedience. That is why this arrangement is usually called the Covenant of Works. Now we enter into the promised bond of blessed communion by means of faith in Jesus and so we enter by way of his exact and entire obedience to the Father. This is usually referred to as the Covenant of Grace, first revealed amid the dust and debris of the fall in Gen 3:15.

Before we transition to a consideration of the person and work of Jesus Christ, God's Son come in the flesh, we should take stock of the ground we have covered. Adam was our federal head and so what he did or did not do was also what we did or did not do. Because Adam failed the ultimate test in the lap of luxury in the Garden of Eden, we suffer guilt, corruption, and alienation as did Adam. Our creaturely status is *not* predicated upon the fall into sin. We are finite creatures, and this is a good thing. By that I mean God pronounced his creation good and indeed very good (Gen 1:4ff). So the fact that we are limited and depen-dent creatures is not in and of itself a bad thing. We are dependent upon God for our existence, our knowledge, and our behavioral standards.[15] Now, subsequent to Adam's first transgression, we also individually and personally are guilty of breaking God's law, both verbally explicit and that written into creation (including being written on our heart), we have become corrupt in our whole nature, and we are alienated from God, our fellow human beings, and our environment.

We should briefly consider the effect of the fall on the human con-dition as it can factor into apologetics. Western philosophy has fixated upon the finitude of man rather than his ethical rebellion against his Creator. This is a hallmark of unbelieving thought, which has some-times seeped into the thought of Christians throughout church history. This is a denial of our *creatureliness* pure and simple. As you no doubt are already realizing, this also implicates human knowledge and behav-ior. The radical denial of our creatureliness means that we are making ourselves into gods and goddesses and denying the God of Scripture. As Paul points out in Rom 1:18–32, this inevitably leads to a denial of

---

15. These correspond to the standard divisions of philosophy into metaphysics or ontology, epistemology, and ethics. These interpenetrate one another so we need to avoid confusing the necessity to focus on one subject at a time (a factor of our finitude) with the idea that these are in fact hermetically compartmentalized realities. They are not.

God's moral expectations of his human creatures. We know what God expects of us but we reject his right to rule us. Now we really are not successful in this rebellion, but we think we are and we like to fool ourselves into thinking we are successful in this endeavor.

As a result of the fall in Adam, there is now a radical breach between thinking based upon God's Word and thinking based in a rebellious rejection of God's Word. This radical breach or "antithesis" is complete *in principle* or at the root but is not complete as it works itself out among individual people.[16] If the antithesis was complete in its personal distribution in our individual human experience, we would cease to exist and would disappear altogether.[17] In addition to the antithesis after the fall, God has instituted the age of common grace as well as saving grace in Christ. As a discerning reader will no doubt note, when Adam and Eve ate from the tree they did not immediately die (Gen 3:7ff). Does that mean that God was ignorant, incompetent, or impotent as Satan through the serpent suggested? Not at all. God institutes common grace, staying the immediate execution of eschatological justice. Common grace provides a *breathing space* between the fall and the consummation in which the gospel is propounded in both the Old Testament and New Testament eras, the outworking of sin is restrained in individuals and society, and God provides for the flourishing of human culture. All of this connects to Christian apologetics in a big way.[18]

---

16. This distinction between the antithesis *in principle* and the *distribution* of the principle in individual human experience, is essential to grasp. The same works with regard to the restoration of the Christian believer. In principle the believer is perfect in Christ and has decisively broken with the powerful corruption of sin. However, the distribution of the principle in individual Christian experience varies from person to person and season of life, etc. See WLC Q&As 77–78 about the distinction between justification and sanctification. Christians are regularly *enjoined* to put off the old man and to put on the new man (Col 3:1–17 and Eph 4:17–5:21) based upon the reality of the believer's union with Christ *in fact*. In other words, sinners cannot be consistent with their God-denial in metaphysics, epistemology, and ethics because they are made in God's image, live in God's world, and are surrounded by his communication and common grace. So also the Christian is not completely consistent with his or her principle because of remaining sin.

17. Another way of saying this is to note that the fall is *ethical* or historical/covenantal and *not* metaphysical.

18. See Cornelius Van Til, *Common Grace and the Gospel.* 2nd ed. (K. Scott Oliphint, ed., Phillipsburg, NJ: P&R Publishing, 2015) and throughout his *Defense of the Faith*, especially ix–x, 3, 7, 13, 21, 171–73, 371, and 383–408. Not to sound trite, but com-

As we have already had occasion to note, God proffered to Adam a transition from his ongoing period of probation should he pass a test of loyalty and obedience. Should he pass the test he would move from a state of changeable or mutable communion to a state of unalloyed eternal blessed communion with God the Father, Son, and Holy Spirit. This is the basis for the statement you sometimes hear in Reformed circles that *eschatology precedes soteriology.* If eschatology is the doctrine of last things how can last things come before salvation? This is so because *protology* or the doctrine of first things and *eschatology* are wrapped up in each other. Now the Covenant of Works in which God proffered to Adam the unending intimate communion bond has been abrogated for us mere mortals. It was *not* abrogated for the other federal head. That brings us to our examination of the person and work of Jesus Christ, whom Paul calls the second Adam or last man (Rom 5:12–21; 1 Cor 15:12–58).

We have already seen that the God of Scripture, and therefore the God of Reformed theology and apologetics, is the Triune God: Father, Son, and Holy Spirit. It is *this* God and *no other* who created Adam and interacted with him as our federal head. It is this God who planned in eternity past to rectify the fall and save a *particular* people for himself (1 Pet 2:4–10). The God who created the universe is the same God who saves. The Father created through speaking the Word (Gen 1:3) and by the hovering of the Spirit (Gen 1:2). The Triune God entered into covenant with Adam and offered him eternal life based upon obedience to the specific prohibition (Gen 2:15–17) of eating from the tree in the middle of the garden. Once Adam disobeyed God the Covenant of Works was no longer operative for Adam or his posterity born by "ordinary generation" (WSC Q&A 16), but if any man was to enter into consummate joyous fellowship with God he must now enter by way of the Covenant of Grace through faith in the other divinely appointed covenant head, Jesus Christ.

Jesus Christ *was and is* the God-man Mediator and Surety of the new covenant.[19] In order to advance the now fallen man to the estate of consummate bliss, God the Father determined to send the Son, who in

---

mon grace is a common theme in the thought and writings of Van Til.

19. A "surety" is someone who guarantees that the conditions of a covenant will be kept.

time (Gal 4:4–5) took to himself a "true body, and a reasonable soul" (WSC Q&A 22) and entered upon a life of experiencing the sin, pain, and miseries of this fallen world. He was *not* himself sinful nor did he have a sinful nature (Heb 4:15; 7:26–28) but he came in the *likeness* of sinful flesh (Rom 8:3) to save those enthralled to Satan and sin and its concomitant miseries, pains, and indeed death.[20] Jesus was not acting as an ordinary private person in what he came to do and in fact did. He was a covenant representative like the first Adam in many ways. Of course, Jesus was unlike Adam in actually obeying his Father and his will. Sinners who by faith believe in Jesus and believe that Jesus lived and died and was raised and ascended for their sin and sins, are united to him and transition as Cornelius Van Til would say, "from wrath to grace" or as the apostle Paul would say, they are transferred from the "kingdom of darkness to the kingdom of the beloved Son" (Col 1:13).

One who is united to Christ by faith is a work under construction. He or she has been buried with Christ and has been raised and indeed ascended with him (Rom 6:1–14; Eph 2:6; Col 3:3). However, this does not mean that the Christian *perfectly* manifests his or her union with Christ (and therefore his or her justification, adoption, definitive, positional, and progressive sanctification) in this life. The Scriptures make it pretty clear that such is not the case. Indeed, one of the things Christians look forward to when the Lord returns is that we will be like him when he reveals himself (1 John 3:1–3). Among other things this means that the Christian is sometimes, in this life, *inconsistent* with what is *actually true* of him or her *in Christ*. In a similar way, the unbeliever is inconsistent with his or her unbelief and suppression of the truth. Many times the unbeliever knows the truth if we think of the specifics of a given fact or series of facts or field of learning or other endeavor.[21] Unbelievers make *intellectually* excellent philosophers, scien-

---

20. I say this to distinguish orthodox Reformed theology from variations of it in the broader Reformed world and in the world of evangelicalism. A Reformed theologian who historically toyed with the idea of Jesus Christ having a sinful nature, albeit while not actually sinning, was the Scottish titan Thomas F. Torrance. More recently Marcus Peter Johnson, *One with Christ: An Evangelical Theology of Salvation* (Wheaton, IL: Crossway, 2013), has advocated for the view.

21. That is, if we think of *discrete facts unto themselves*, or as they exist in *isolation from* the Triune God of Scripture and his plan for the universe and its history, an unbeliever can know things very well indeed. This is what we call mental abstraction. We

tists, butchers, bakers, candle stick makers, and even theologians. This is closely tied with common grace and what has historically been called "civic righteousness."

The Christian longingly anticipates the return of Jesus Christ. He or she lives in the light of the coming of the King of kings and Lord of lords in all his glory with the heavenly hosts trailing behind. While in principle the Christian has already attained to the consummate communion with the Triune God by means of union with Christ (what Adam would have attained had he been obedient to God in the garden), his or her full enjoyment of this unbreakable bond will not occur until the saint either comes with the Lord or, if he or she is still alive, is transformed in an instant at Christ's *parousia*. The book of Hebrews gets at this reality when it talks about God's people entering into their Sabbath rest. The author is not talking about their rest from fruitless works in trying to merit God's favor. That is a given. What the author of Hebrews is getting at is the Sabbath rest that awaits the people of God at Christ's return. In principle, the Christian possesses eternal life already, but the full enjoyment awaits the return of the Savior.[22]

Between the time a sinner believes on Christ and is transformed into a saint, and his or her full transformation at Christ's return if alive at that time, or comes with the Lord along with the angels in glory, the Christian is called to follow Christ and share the reason for his hope (1 Pet 3:15) with unbelievers. All Christians are called to do apologetics. Just as all Christians are to share the gospel of Jesus Christ as the Lord provides opportunities. In both apologetics and evangelism there is a

---

focus in on one fact or a limited series of facts. But if we were to widen our view to include the relationship of each fact in the universe and the relationship of these discrete facts to the laws of nature and the relation of these to God, in this sense the unbeliever *does not* and *cannot know* the truth about discrete facts as these facts actually exist and relate to their universe. The truth of the matter is that facts are what they are by virtue of God's plan for them. When we deny the connection between these facts and the Triune God and his will/plan then we must find a substitute to ground these facts and/ or arbitrarily grind our intellectual queries to a screeching halt.

22. I should say that we enter into the *fullest* enjoyment of our unbreakable communion bond with the Triune God not at our deaths but when the Lord returns. The WSC Q&As 22 and 23 get at this when they note that the soul of the deceased saint is made perfect in holiness at his death and he immediately enters into glory, while it is not until the resurrection when the resurrected bodies of saints are reunited with their souls which have been with the Lord in heaven in the intermediate state, that they experience the *full enjoyment* of God forever.

general requirement that rests on the church *as a whole* and there is a special gifting to those *individually called* to do apologetics and evangelism full time.[23] In this era of antithesis and common grace and in this era of the overlap of this present evil age with the coming age of righteousness and joy,[24] we are called to defend the faith and confront unbelief in all its varied forms.

Elements of a Reformed Covenantal Apologetic

Covenantal apologetics involves three basic steps arising from the theology explicated above. Christianity is *not* simply the best religion among many contenders, it is the only true faith *whatsoever*. Apologetics involves careful attention given to the position of your opponent. If your interlocutor cannot recognize himself or herself in your give and take, then you need to go back to the drawing board. You are seeking to persuade the unbeliever of what the late apologist Greg Bahnsen called the "impossibility of the contrary."[25] That is, you are seeking to show that

---

23. This would be primarily, if not exclusively, ordained ministers of the gospel. This is not the place to get into the fully Reformed understanding of church life and evangelism. Suffice it to say that the general evangelical expectation that the full weight of the Great Commission rests on every individual Christian is an assumption rather than well-founded doctrine. In Matt 28:19–20 the risen Christ commands the apostles to go into all the world making disciples by means of baptism and teaching. This was a command issued to the church *as a whole* through those holding the *extraordinary office* of apostle. The obligation of that command devolves upon the *regular officers* of the church (i.e., ministers and elders) now, especially ministers as obedience to this command involves teaching and the administration of baptism. The command to do apologetics differs in that it was *not* issued to church officers *only* as was the Great Commission.

24. This overlap of the ages is frequently found in Paul and other portions of God's Word. For instance, Jesus calls attention to this drawing back into history the end-times judgment in his person and work in John 11 in his conversation with Martha about the death and resurrection of her deceased brother Lazarus. The overlap of this present evil age and the age to come occurs between the first and second comings of Jesus. This involves, among other things, an intensification of the antithesis that begins after the fall (Genesis 3:15). For a masterful apologetic development of the antithesis, see Augustine, *The City of God Against the Pagans*. Cambridge Studies of the History of Political Thought series (R. W. Dyson, tr. and ed., Cambridge, UK: Cambridge University Press, 1998). For a helpful study of the apologetic significance of the overlap of the ages, see William D. Dennison, *Paul's Two Age Construction and Apologetics* (Eugene, OR: Wipf & Stock, 2000) and more recently a published collection of a variety of his essays, *In Defense of the Eschaton: Essays on Reformed Apologetics* (James Baird, ed., Eugene, OR: Wipf & Stock, 2015).

25. See Greg Bahnsen, *Van Til's Apologetic: Readings and Analysis* (Phillipsburg, NJ:

your opponent's views do not hold together and cannot work in the way
he or she thinks they do. The first step of the covenantal approach involves what is usually called the *internal critique*. After you demonstrate
the internal incoherence and make evident the cracks in the foundation
you then move to the *external critique*. In the external critique you bring
the claims of Christian truth into direct collision with the views of the
unbeliever. Folks who are new to the apologetic task often jump to the
external critique thinking they have completed their work. This is only
one third of the task. Finally, you need to bring the *unbeliever to Christ*
or, perhaps more accurately, you need to bring *Christ to the unbeliever*.
Apologetics, like preaching and evangelism, is intended to present the
claims of our Lord to the unbeliever and calling, in a gentle but firm
manner (per 1 Pet 3:15), for a response. This whole defense may take
more than one encounter.

The internal critique, or what Dr. Van Til referred to as "standing
upon the ground of your opponent for argument's sake," is key to any
apologetic defense.[26] Here you seek to deconstruct the unbelieving
worldview from the inside. This obviously requires that you properly
understand your opponent's position or aim to gain clarity in your give
and take. Creating straw men or inaccurate caricatures leads nowhere.
You must also carefully distinguish between the logical trajectory of
your opponent's view and what implications he or she personally owns.
That is, do not attribute to your conversation partner views he or she
does not actually embrace. It is fair to point out where the logic of a position inexorably leads, but we must recognize, as we noted above, that
people are not always consistent with their first principles.

The external critique or "getting your opponent to stand on Christian ground for arguments sake" is your opportunity to show how the
Christian faith truthfully and truly addresses concerns expressed in your
opponent's false views.[27] It is not just that Christianity does a better job
answering your opponent's concerns. The Christian faith is the only

---

P&R Publishing, 1998).

26. Van Til, *Defense of the Faith*, 121–127. I cite this passage, but similar things are
said throughout the Van Til literary corpus. One the best tools for researching through
the breadth and depth of Van Til is *The Works of Cornelius Van Til, 1895–1987* CD–
ROM (Eric Sigward, ed. New York, NY: Army Labels Co., 1997). This is currently
available through the Logos electronic library program.

27. Van Til, *Defense of the Faith*, 121–127.

true and faithful way your opponent's concerns will ever be addressed since the Christian faith reflects the real world as it is and not just as we wish it would be.

Finally, apologetics is about defending the Christian faith against criticisms while also offering a critique of false philosophies and compromising forms of the Christian faith. While it is true that apologetics is concerned with dealing with primarily intellectual questions, you are dealing with real flesh and blood people with sinful wills and emotions too. The Christian faith is a whole-souled faith that addresses the whole person.[28] Moreover, the Christian faith is about the Lord Jesus Christ in the final analysis. This whole apologetic encounter involves reminding people, anywhere in the world, of the God they know through natural revelation written into the vary fiber of their being. We are called to bring the claims of King Jesus to people and call for their surrender. Yet we do this in a gentle and respectful manner. Be truthful, be relentless. But however long and winding the path you follow, it needs to lead to the feet of Jesus. And Jesus' feet are nail-scarred, as are his hands and his side is spear-pierced. Christ just may use us, in the power of the Holy Spirit, to persuade an unbeliever to trust Jesus Christ for salvation.

Conclusion

While there are many ways Christians have sought to defend their faith to the unbelieving world, at the end of the day, that apologetic defense will reflect the theology of the apologist whether he or she intends it to or not.[29] As Reformed Christians we believe that the Reformed expression of the faith *just is* biblical Christianity. Our defense of the faith ought and needs to reflect this biblical view. Our apologetic method

28. See Paul Helseth, *"Right Reason" and Princeton Mind: An Unorthodox Proposal* (Phillipsburg, NJ: P&R Publishing, 2010) and related articles on how the faculty at Princeton Theological Seminary between 1812 and 1929 understood right reason to be regenerate reason, *not* neutral reasoning. In other words, subsequent to the fall, the only *properly functioning* reasoning process is manifested in those who are united to Christ and whose intellect, will, and emotions are *in principle*, being progressively restored. The mind was never meant to function properly apart from properly functioning wills and emotions.

29. There is no *generic* Christian apologetic approach. If you follow a lowest common denominator approach, you have abstracted the Christian faith at that point and the faith commended bears no resemblance to the faith held by anyone. Even C. S. Lewis believed more than he wrote down in his *Mere Christianity*.

is and ought to be grounded in the theology which comes to us from the Scriptures. I have sought to elucidate the contours of the Reformed faith as it bears on the apologetic task and then briefly outline the task itself. May the Triune God be glorified in our efforts to defend the faith on the ground of a biblical Christianity.

Related Episodes

- Christian Theistic Evidences with K. Scott Oliphint
  » http://reformedforum.org/ctc429
- Van Til's Common Grace and the Gospel with K. Scott Oliphint
  » http://reformedforum.org/ctc399
- Covenantal Apologetics Colloquim
  » http://reformedforum.org/events/2015-apologetics-colloquium
- Paul's Two Age Construction and Apologetics
  » http://reformedforum.org/ctc92
- Covenantal Apologetics and Common-Sense Realism with Nathaniel Gray Sutanto
  » http://reformedforum.org/ctc368
- The Trinity, Image of God, and Apologetics: Bavinck's Consistently Reformed Defense of the Faith, James J. Cassidy
  » http://reformedforum.org/rf16_02_cassidy
- Covenantal Apologetics with K. Scott Oliphint
  » http://reformedforum.org/ctc289
- A Comparison of Rahnerian to Reformed Apologetics
  » http://reformedforum.org/ctc74
- Apologetics and Islam with James White
  » http://reformedforum.org/ctc44
- In Defense of the Eschaton with Bill Dennison
  » http://reformedforum.org/ctc413
- Jesus Christ as Apologist with Brian DeJong
  » http://reformedforum.org/ctc395
- The Nature and Use of Apologetic Evidences
  » http://reformedforum.org/ctc288
- Reasons for Faith with K. Scott Oliphint
  » http://reformedforum.org/ctc264
- The Defense of the Faith with K. Scott Oliphint
  » http://reformedforum.org/ctc36

Suggested Reading List

People often ask us to recommend books. While the occasional inquirer asks about a specific issue, most simply seek general guidance in beginning a Reformed program of learning. There are so many good books to read! But we have to begin somewhere. We have found that having a well organized and thorough reading plan promotes discipline and forces the reader to have a breadth of knowledge that will enrich the reader's studies in all areas. Our list is ambitious, but slightly skewed. For instance, our church history section is heavy on American history, since—for better or worse—our constituency is overwhelmingly American. Also, this list is in progress. We will add items, remove others, and move things around as new books are published and we receive feedback.

Several of these suggestions come from the Westminster Theological Seminary recommended reading list, which we encourage you to review. It is also important to familiarize yourself with the Westminster Confession of Faith and Catechisms. The Orthodox Presbyterian Church have made these available online in a variety of formats. But above all, and we cannot stress this highly enough, prayerfully read your Bible regularly in such a manner that you work through all of Scripture—preferably at least once each year. Theological study is worthless—even detrimental—apart from a life spent in prayer and reading God's Word.

How to Use this List

Within each discipline, the readings are divided into three categories corresponding to when it would be appropriate to read them. This does not always correspond to difficulty. Occasionally, a level three work will be stylistically accessible but simply would not be applicable until you have worked through the content in the level one and two works. We have also attempted to list the titles within a given level in a suggested reading order. Nonetheless, each reader has a unique experience and particular acumen, so these suggestions should be viewed with a measure of flexibility.

Readers new to the Reformed tradition may find even these first level books quite challenging, but be strong and courageous. Keep working hard and asking questions. After mastering the first level material, move to the second level books. Since the disciplines inform one another, it is important to build a wide foundation before moving to the next level. Therefore, complete the level one material in every discipline before moving to any of the second levels. Likewise, move to the third levels only after you have a firm grasp on all of the intermediate material. This is not a race. You will benefit much more by careful, patient, and deliberate reading. Think quality, not quantity.

Biblical Studies & Hermeneutics

Level 1

Ridderbos, Herman N. *Redemptive History and the New Testament Scriptures*. Phillipsburg, N.J.: P&R Publishing, 1988.
Poythress, Vern S. *God-Centered Biblical Interpretation*. Phillipsburg, N.J.: P&R Pub., 1999.
Carson, D. A., and Douglas J. Moo. *An Introduction to the New Testament*. 2nd ed. Zondervan, 2005.

Level 2

Beale, G. K. *The Erosion of Inerrancy in Evangelicalism.* Wheaton, IL: Crossway, 2008.

Poythress, Vern S. *Understanding Dispensationalists.* Phillipsburg, N.J.: P&R Publishing, 1993.

Gaffin, Jr., Richard B. "The Redemptive-Historical View." In *Biblical Hermeneutics: Five Views,* edited by Stanley E Porter and Beth M. Stovell. Downers Grove, Ill.: IVP Academic, 2012.

Level 3

Vos, Geerhardus. *Redemptive History and Biblical Interpretation: The Shorter Writings of Geerhardus Vos.* Edited by Richard B. Gaffin, Jr. Phillipsburg N.J.: P&R Publishing, 2001.

Tipton, Lane G. "The Gospel and Redemptive-Historical Hermeneutics." In *Confident of Better Things: Essays Commemorating Seventy-Five Years of the Orthodox Presbyterian Church,* edited by John R. Muether and Danny E. Olinger. Willow Grove, PA: The Committee on Christian Education for the Orthodox Presbyterian Church, 2011.

Ridderbos, Herman. *The Gospel of John: A Theological Commentary.* Wm. B. Eerdmans Publishing Company, 1997.

Biblical Theology

Level 1

Vos, Geerhardus. *Grace and Glory: Sermons Preached in the Chapel of Princeton Theological Seminary.* Grand Rapids Mich.: The Reformed Press, 1922.

Ridderbos, Herman N. *When the Time Had Fully Come: Studies in New Testament Theology.* Wipf & Stock Publishers, 2001.

Poythress, Vern. *The Shadow of Christ in the Law of Moses.* Phillipsburg, New Jersey: Presbyterian and Reformed Publishing Company, 1995.

Level 2

Vos, Geerhardus. *Biblical Theology: Old and New Testaments.* Carlisle, PA: Banner of Truth, 2000.

Kline, Meredith G. *Kingdom Prologue: Genesis Foundations for a Covenantal Worldview.* Wipf & Stock Publishers, 2006.

Ridderbos, Herman. *The Coming of the Kingdom.* Edinburgh: Christian World Publications, 1979.

Vos, Geerhardus. *The Kingdom of God and the Church.* Presbyterian & Reformed Pub Co, 1972.

Level 3

Vos, Geerhardus. *The Pauline Eschatology.* P&R Publishing, 1979.

Beale, G. K. *A New Testament Biblical Theology.* Grand Rapids, MI: Baker, 2011.

Vos, Geerhardus. *The Teaching of the Epistle to the Hebrews.* Grand Rapids: W.B. Eerdmans Pub. Co., 1956.

Systematic Theology

Level 1

Ferguson, Sinclair B. *The Christian Life: A Doctrinal Introduction.* Banner of Truth, 1981.

Murray, John. *Redemption, Accomplished and Applied.* Grand Rapids: W.B. Eerdmans Pub. Co., 1955.

Warfield, B. B. *The Inspiration and Authority of the Bible.* Philadelphia, Pa.: Presbyterian and Reformed Pub. Co, 1948.

Young, E. J. *Thy Word is Truth.* Carlisle, PA: Banner of Truth, 1963.

Warfield, Benjamin Breckinridge. *The Plan of Salvation.* Boonton, NJ: Simpson Pub. Co., 1989.

Level 2

Calvin, John. *Institutes of the Christian Religion.* Wm. B. Eerdmans Publishing Company, 1990.

Murray, John. *Collected Writings of John Murray.* Four volumes. Edinburgh: Banner of Truth Trust, 1977.

Gaffin, Jr. Richard B. *Resurrection and Redemption*. Phillipsburg, NJ: P&R Publishing, 1987.

Ferguson, Sinclair. *The Holy Spirit*. Downers Grove, IL: InterVarsity, 1997.

Kline, Meredith G. *Images of the Spirit*. Eugene, Ore.: Wipf and Stock Publishers, 1999. (This could also easily fall under biblical theology.)

Level 3

Bavinck, Herman. *Reformed Dogmatics*, four volumes. Edited by John Bolt. Translated by John Vriend. Baker Academic, 2003–2008.

Oliphint, K. Scott, ed. *Justified In Christ: God's Plan for Us in Justification*. Mentor, 2007.

Ridderbos, Herman N. *Paul: An Outline of His Theology*. Wm. B. Eerdmans Publishing Company, 1977.

Van Til, Cornelius. *Introduction to Systematic Theology: Prolegomena and the Doctrines of Revelation, Scripture, and God*. 2nd ed. P&R Publishing, 2007.

Apologetics & Philosophy

Level 1

Machen, J. Gresham. *Christianity and Liberalism*. Grand Rapids, Michigan: William B. Eerdmans Publishing Co., 2009.

Oliphint, K. Scott. *The Battle Belongs to the Lord*. Phillipsburg, New Jersey: Phillipsburg, New Jersey: P&R Publishing, 2003.

Pratt, Richard. *Every Thought Captive: A Study Manual for the Defense of Christian Truth*. Phillipsburg N.J.: Presbyterian and Reformed Pub. Co., 1979.

Bahnsen, Greg L. *Always Ready: Directions for Defending the Faith*. Covenant Media Press, 1996.

Level 2

Oliphint, K. Scott. *Covenantal Apologetics: Principles and Practice in Defense of Our Faith*. Wheaton, Illinois: Crossway, 2013.

Van Til, Cornelius and Greg L. Bahnsen, ed. *Van Til's Apologetic:*

Readings and Analysis. Phillipsburg, New Jersey: P&R Publishing, 1998.

Van Til, Cornelius with annotations by K. Scott Oliphint. *The Defense of the Faith.* Phillipsburg, New Jersey: P&R Publishing, 2008.

Oliphint, K. Scott, and Lane G. Tipton, eds. *Revelation and Reason: New Essays in Reformed Apologetics.* Phillipsburg, New Jersey: P&R Publishing, 2007.

Bahnsen, Greg. *Presuppositional Apologetics: Stated and Defended.* Powder Springs Ga.; Nacogdoches Tex.: American Vision Inc.; Covenant Media Press, 2008.

Level 3

Oliphint, K. Scott. Reasons for Faith: Philosophy in the Service of Theology. Phillipsburg, NJ: Presbyterian and Reformed Publishing Company, 2006.

Jones, W. T. A History of Western Philosophy, five volumes. You can save large amounts of money (e.g. $100 vs. $2) by buying these used from sites like bookfinder.com or abebooks.com. They are often assigned as textbooks in universities, and students tend to sell them at the end of each semester.

Church History & Historical Theology

Level 1

Chadwick, Henry. *The Early Church.* Harmondsworth: Penguin, 1993.

Wilken, Robert Louis. *The Spirit of Early Christian Thought: Seeking the Face of God.* Yale University Press, 2005.

Lindberg, Carter. *The European Reformations.* Oxford, OX, UK; Cambridge, Mass., USA: Blackwell Publishers, 1996.

Hart, D. G., and John R. Muether. *Seeking a Better Country: 300 Years of American Presbyterianism.* P & R Publishing, 2007.

Hart, D. G. *Deconstructing Evangelicalism: Conservative Protestantism in the Age of Billy Graham.* Grand Rapids MI: Baker Academic, 2004.

100

Level 2

Kelly, J. N. D. *Early Christian Doctrines*. San Francisco: HarperSanFrancisco, 1978.

Pelikan, Jaroslav. *The Emergence of the Catholic Tradition*. Chicago: University of Chicago Press, 1975.

MacCulloch, Diarmaid. *The Reformation: A History*. Viking Adult, 2004.

Noll, Mark A. *America's God: From Jonathan Edwards to Abraham Lincoln*. New Ed. Oxford University Press, USA, 2005.

Level 3

Muller, Richard A. *Post-Reformation Reformed Dogmatics: The Rise and Development of Reformed Orthodoxy, Ca. 1520 to Ca. 1725*. 2nd ed. 4 volumes. Grand Rapids Mich: Baker Academic, 2003.

Ahlstrom, Sydney E. *A Religious History of the American People*. New Haven: Yale University Press, 2004.

Livingston, James C., Francis Schüssler Fiorenza, Sarah Coakley, and James H. Evans Jr. *Modern Christian Thought: The Twentieth Century*. 2nd ed. Fortress Press, 2006.

Practical Theology

Level 1

Clowney, Edmund P. *Called to the Ministry*. Phillipsburg, NJ: Presbyterian and Reformed Publishing, 1976.

Warfield, B.B. *The Religious Life of Theological Students*. Phillipsburg, NJ: Presbyterian and Reformed Publishing.

Lane, Tim and Paul Tripp. *How People Change*. Greensboro, NC: New Growth Press, 2008.

Level 2

Hart, D. G., and John R. Muether. *With Reverence and Awe: Returning to the Basics of Reformed Worship*. P&R Publishing, 2002.

Powlison, David. *Seeing With New Eyes*. Phillipsburg, NJ: Presbyterian and Reformed Publishing, 2003.

Welch, Ed. *Blame It On the Brain*. Phillipsburg, NJ: Presbyterian and Reformed Publishing, 1998.

Johnson, Dennis. *Him We Proclaim: Preaching Christ from All the Scriptures*. Phillipsburg, NJ: P&R Pub., 2007.

Level 3

Powlison, David. *The Biblical Counseling Movement*. Greensboro, NC: New Growth Press, 2010.

Murray, John. *Principles of Conduct: Aspects of Biblical Ethics*. Grand Rapids Mich.: W.B. Eerdmans Pub., 1957.

Robinson, Stuart. *The Church of God as an Essential Element of the Gospel, and the Idea, Structure, and Functions Thereof. A Discourse in Four Parts*. Willow Grove Pa.: Committee on Christian Education of the Orthodox Presbyterian Church, 2009.

Classics, &tc.

Many of these titles are recognized Christian classics and/or foundational works for contemporary Reformed thought. As such, they are important works to read for historical breadth and sensitivity. Many different editions of these titles are available, including electronic editions, which are often available for free in Amazon's Kindle Store.

Level 1

Dennison, James T. *Reformed Confessions of the 16th and 17th Centuries in English Translation: Volume I, 1523–1552*. Grand Rapids, Mich.: Reformation Heritage Books, 2008.

Augustine. *The Confessions*. New Ed. New City Press, 2003. (There are also various paperback editions available.)

Luther, Martin, J. I Packer, and O. R. Johnston. *The Bondage of the Will*. Old Tappan, NJ: Revell, 1957.

Level 2

Anselm. *Anselm of Canterbury: The Major Works*. Edited by Brian Davies and G. R. Evans. Oxford; New York: Oxford University Press, 1998.

Owen, John, and W. H. Goold, ed. *The Works of John Owen*. London:

Banner of Truth Trust, 1965. Focus on volumes six and ten.

Level 3

Augustine. *The City of God*. Penguin Classics, 2004.

Edwards, Jonathan. *The Religious Affections*. New Haven: Yale University Press, 1959.

About the Authors

Camden M. Bucey

Camden graduated from Bradley University and then worked at Caterpillar, Inc. in Peoria, Illinois for several years before moving to Philadelphia to attend Westminster Theological Seminary. He earned an MDiv and a PhD in Historical and Theological Studies (concentrating in Systematic Theology) from Westminster. His dissertation addressed Karl Rahner's doctrine of divine self-communication. In April 2013, Camden was ordained and installed as the pastor of Hope Orthodox Presbyterian Church in Grayslake, Illinois. He also serves as an adjunct faculty member at Mid-America Reformed Seminary in Dyer, Indiana. Camden is married to Erica, and they have three sons.

James J. Cassidy

Jim was installed in July of 2014 as a church planter at South Austin Presbyterian Church. The mission of the new church is to establish a faithful Presbyterian church in South Austin with an emphasis on Christ-centered preaching and distinctly Reformed worship.

Jim was raised in a Roman Catholic home in Edison, New Jersey. He was later led to the Lord by a friend in his sophomore year of college. He has since then come to understand the wonderful Doctrines of Grace by God's kindness. His wife was raised in Madison, New Jersey and was led to the Lord through the ministry of Grace OPC in Westfield, New Jersey. She is a busy and active mother who is involved in the teaching ministry of the church as well as various events in our community. He believes that the doctrines of the Reformation are the clearest expression of biblical truth and provide answers for a world lost in sin and suffering. He is committed to proclaiming Christ and him crucified from all the Scriptures. Jim earned an MDiv at Westminster Theological Seminary as well as the PhD in Historical and Theological Studies, concentrating in Systematic Theology.

Glen J. Clary

Glen graduated from Southwestern Christian University in Oklahoma City with a bachelor's degree in biblical studies. He earned an MDiv from Westminster Theological Seminary, and a DMin in the field of Reformed worship from Erskine Theological Seminary where he studied under Hughes Oliphant Old. Glen is a minister in the Orthodox Presbyterian Church. He pastored Immanuel Orthodox Presbyterian Church in West Collingswood, NJ from 2005–2012, and he currently pastors Providence Presbyterian Church in Pflugerville, Texas. Glen teaches Reformed worship for the Ministerial Training Institute of the OPC. He is married to Cathe, and they have seven children.

Lane G. Tipton

Lane holds the Charles Krahe Chair of Systematic Theology and is associate professor of systematic theology at Westminster Theological Seminary. He also serves as the pastor of Trinity Orthodox Presbyterian Church in Easton, Pennsylvania. Lane earned an MDiv from Westminster Seminary California and a PhD from Westminster Theological Seminary where he wrote a dissertation on Cornelius Van Til's Trinitarian theology. His academic interests are many, including hermeneutics, soteriology, Christology, covenant theology, Trinitarian theology, modern theology, and the integration of biblical and systematic theology.

Lane is married and has four children.

Jeffrey C. Waddington

Jeff came to faith in Christ in 1983 having been raised in a Christian home. When he came to faith in Christ, he also sensed a call to ministry and in his context, that involved service as a minister in a Wesleyan-Arminian denomination. Jeff served as a pastor for eight years from 1986 to 1994 and after that time became Reformed. Shortly thereafter Jeff was exposed to the writings of Cornelius Van Til and saw his apologetic method as the natural outgrowth of Reformed theology. In 1997 Jeff and his family moved to Philadelphia, PA so that he could commence his MDiv studies at Westminster Theological Seminary. Jeff graduated from that program in 2000 and then began the PhD program in Historical and Theological Studies with an emphasis in Apologetics. He graduated in 2013.

Jeff's interests are legion, but he is especially interested in epistemology, systematics, biblical and historical theology. Jeff's special area of focus is the philosophical theology of Jonathan Edwards. In addition to his academic pursuits Jeff served as an intern in the Presbyterian Church in America before moving over to the Orthodox Presbyterian Church. Jeff serves as stated supply at Knox Orthodox Presbyterian Church in Lansdown, Pennsylvania. Jeff has been married since 1990 and has two wonderful daughters.

Scripture Index

CPSIA information can be obtained
at www.ICGtesting.com
Printed in the USA
BVOW04s1941220317
479182BV00002B/4/P